THE
APPLE A DAY
COOKBOOK

Janet Reeves

NIMBUS
PUBLISHING

To Helen Murphy, my mother,
the wonderful woman who
taught me the joy of preparing
and sharing good food.

Nimbus Publishing Limited
3731 Mackintosh St, Halifax, NS B3K 5A5
(902) 455-4286 nimbus.ca

Printed and bound in Canada

Design: Trina Tucker

Library and Archives Canada Cataloguing in Publication

Reeves, Janet, 1942-
The apple a day cookbook / Janet Reeves.
ISBN 978-1-55109-858-6
1. Cooking (Apples). 2. Cookbooks. I. Title.

TX813.A6R43 2011   641.6'411   C2011-903906-0

Originally published by Ragweed Press

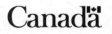  

Nimbus Publishing acknowledges the financial support for its publishing activities from the Government of Canada through the Canada Book
Fund (CBF) and the Canada Council for the Arts, and from the Province
of Nova Scotia through the Department of Communities, Culture and
Heritage.

The History of the Apple

Apples are thought to have originated in the Caucasus Mountains in western Asia. They may have been the first cultivated fruit, and knowledge of them goes back to the Stone Age. Sketches of apples have been found on the rocky walls of the homes of early cave dwellers. These first apples were most likely quite small, hard, and bitter varieties, much like today's crab apples. Scientists think the modern apple (larger and sweeter) resulted from centuries of crossbreeding and the cultivation of different wild trees.

We do know that the modern apple tree was flourishing at the beginning of recorded history. There is evidence that people have been trimming apple trees for thousands of years, and that some varieties have been recognized and propagated for at least two thousand years in Europe: carbonized apples, cut for drying and thought to be between ten thousand and fifteen thousand years old, have been found by archaeologists in the remains of prehistoric Swiss and Italian lake dwellings. Apple seeds, called pips, have even been found in Egyptian pyramids.

The early Greeks were growing apples by the year 4 BC, and developed the technique of grafting. A twig from a desirable tree would be grafted and develop its own set of roots to produce a fruit exactly like that of the mother tree. The Romans developed at least twenty-five varieties of apples, and were the first recorded people to preserve apples by dropping them whole into pots of honey. Some of our recipes for apples have even been passed down to us from the Middle Ages, adapted over the years for more modern kitchens.

The apple is a good traveller. Primitive people ate wild apples and threw away the cores, causing seeds to germinate and new trees to begin. Birds and wildlife also spread the apple, much as they still do today. One has only to take a country walk to find many wild apple trees.

The apple has travelled from southwest Asia, through China, Babylon, and Europe, and finally across the sea to the Americas and all other parts of the globe. An ancient Viking ship, raised from the bottom of the sea off the coast of Norway, contained buckets of apples. Spanish explorers also carried apples to Mexico and South America. The first apples to arrive in England are thought to have come from the apple cores dropped by Roman soldiers when Julius Caesar conquered Britain.

The first record of apple seeds in North America occurs in the early seventeenth century in Massachusetts, the birthplace of Johnny Appleseed,

Introduction

The apple is our favourite fruit: there are thousands of varieties in North America alone, and it is the best-known and most widely distributed tree fruit in the world. Indeed, 90 percent of North American families eat apples regularly. Apples are also one of the most versatile fruits on today's market: they can be served in more fashions and combinations than any other.

Perhaps the apple is so popular because we find it to be the perfect food, appealing to all five senses. It has a pleasant aroma, is sweet to taste, has a resounding crunch and a pretty colour, and is smooth to the touch. Moreover, it is economical, nutritious, and delicious, readily available, and easy to prepare in an endless number of culinary delights.

The Apple a Day Cookbook is a celebration of this hardy and versatile fruit that has migrated from the remote Caucasus Mountains into every corner of the world. In the pages that follow, I have included historical and nutritional information, folklore, helpful hints, and illustrations, as well as nearly three hundred tried-and-true apple recipes, both old and new. You will find international favourites, traditional standbys, and the newest apple delights from around the world. All the recipes have been tested in my own kitchen and at my table, and are presented in imperial measurements that can be easily expanded or reduced. The recipes are adapted for modern kitchens, yet contain the same basic foods used by our pioneer ancestors and require no special equipment or ingredients. Although I've recommended a specific variety of apple for some recipes, I would encourage cooks to try different combinations, experimenting to satisfy individual tastes.

Above all, the researching and writing of this book has been a most enjoyable and rewarding experience. I hope all those who open its pages will be similarly rewarded, and I dedicate it to everyone who loves good food.

Acknowledgements

The author wishes to give special thanks to the following individuals and organizations who generously provided essential information, recipes, help, and encouragement: Dr. Craig Williams, Summerside, PEI; Michael Sanders, BC Ministry of Agriculture; Janice Lutz and the Nova Scotia Fruit Growers Association, Kentville, NS; Scotian Gold Co-op Ltd., Kentville, NS; Apple Auto Glass, Summerside, PEI; Betty Howatt, Howatt's Fruit Farm, Tryon, PEI; Bert and Willie Hekman, Cackleberry Farms, PEI; Gayle and Denny Hopping, Gaylden Orchard, Mills Point, PEI; Ontario Apple Growers; BC Tree Fruits Ltd., Kelowna, BC; New Brunswick Apple Marketing Board; Canada Pork Inc.; Ontario Wheat Producers' Marketing Board; Inga-Lill Harding, California; Hilary Montgomery, Ireland; PEI Department of Agriculture; the Apple Blossom Festival Committee, Cornwallis, NS; Communications Branch, Agriculture Canada; Shirley Doucette, Miscouche, PEI; Deciduous Fruit Board, Bellville, South Africa; Fresh for Flavour Foundation, Ottawa, Ont.; Lorene Waugh, Komoka, Ont.; Agriculture, Fisheries and Food Products Branch, Industry, Science and Technology Canada, Ottawa, Ont.; British Columbia Orchard Industry Museum, Kelowna, BC; Summerside Lending Library, PEI.

Special thanks to Mary Pickett, of Kelvin Grove, PEI, and Sheila Compton of Compton's Vegetable, for supplying apples; to Kelly Amos for help in recipe testing; to Adam DeWitt, for his invaluable help in peeling bucket after bucket of apples; to my brother Terry Murphy of Windsor, Ont.; to our daughter Marina, and daughter-in-law Stacey for help with research; to my husband, Allison, for his loving encouragement; and to all those who contributed anecdotes, recipes, and much-needed support.

Contents

more than a century before his birth. As each new frontier was established in America, apples from settlers' motherlands were planted and nurtured.

Long before the Spanish explorers, Julius Caesar, the European settlers, and Johnny Appleseed, however, the apple played a significant part in the mythology and traditions of the most ancient nations. Apples are mentioned in the Bible, in the Hindu Code of Manu, and in the Egyptian Book of the Dead.

There is much fascinating mythology and folklore about this oldest known fruit. The best-known legend in the Western tradition is that of Eve in the Garden of Eden being tempted by the serpent and in turn tempting Adam with an apple. The Bible, however, does not mention the apple specifically, but simply states, "the tree of knowledge of good and evil" (Genesis 2:16). Maybe this phrase, "good and evil," is why the apple has been associated with both good and evil qualities. In fact, the fruit used by Eve was probably not an apple, but an apricot or a quince—apples do not flourish well in the hot, dry climate of the Near East.

Early Christian legends and Greek mythology about the apple have many points of similarity. Apples were symbols of love, beauty, and goodness in both traditions. One story from Greek mythology I particularly like recounts how an apple caused the Trojan War. The goddess of discord, Eris, was not invited to a banquet celebrating the wedding of Peleus and Thetis. Eris, reputed to be the mother of all lies, battles, and murders, came to the party uninvited and determined to cause trouble. She picked a golden apple and labelled it "For the Fairest." Then she rolled the apple onto the table between the attending goddesses. Each goddess thought the apple was for her, and an argument erupted. Paris, a young mortal man, was asked to judge who was the fairest. Each goddess tried to bribe Paris and promised him a reward if he chose her. Paris's final judgement took place at Mount Ida, with the goddesses Athena, Hera, and Aphrodite taking part. Aphrodite, the goddess of love, had promised Paris the hand of Helen of Troy should he choose her, and Paris, who desired Helen of Troy, agreed to Aphrodite's bribe. She received the golden apple and Paris got his wish. Unfortunately, Helen was already married to Menelaus. King Menelaus marched on Troy and the Trojan War began. In the end, all the Trojans were killed and Helen was reunited with her husband.

Another popular legend features Aphrodite and Atlanta, the first great woman athlete. Atlanta had exceptional ability as a hunter and runner. She had been told by an oracle that she would become mortal and die if she were ever to marry. Atlanta's father, however, wanted very much to see his daughter married and she did not want to displease him. She promised to marry any man who could outrun her in a foot race; but any man who lost the race would have to die. Hippomenes was in love with the beautiful Atlanta but knew he could not outrun her. He prayed to the goddess of love, Aphrodite, for help, and she answered his prayer by giving him three golden apples. The race began and Atlanta, by far the faster runner, soon was ahead. Hippomenes threw a golden apple into her path. Atlanta stopped to pick up and admire the apple, giving Hippomenes time to catch up. This happened three times, once for each apple, and Hippomenes won the race.

From the beginning, apples have been associated with magical and healing powers. As early as 35 BC, people would bounce apple seeds to pick out the person they would marry. In the sixth century, apples were considered a health food and used specifically for stomach problems. In 1398, it was written that "Chyldren loved an apple more than golde," and apples were thought to be the most easily digested food. Today's applesauce still has this reputation. By the fifteenth century, apples were used as laxatives, and in the sixteenth century they were thought to erase the scarring of smallpox. In the seventeenth century it was thought that apples cured tuberculosis; in the eighteenth, that they were a cure for sore throats, and in the nineteenth century that they eased the pain of rheumatism. This belief has carried into the present—apples are ordered for the treatment of gout, anaemia, and arthritis.

The Halloween tradition of dunking for apples began as an Irish custom of finding your true love. Apples were marked with the names of would-be suitors and floated in a pan of water. A blindfolded woman would try to catch an apple in her teeth; whichever one she caught would bear the name of her future husband. In Ireland today, there still exists a Halloween custom of peeling an apple in one long peeling and throwing the peel over your shoulder. When it falls, it will be in the shape of the initial of your true love. If the apple peel breaks, you will remain single.

The story I like best is that of the apple's rejuvenating powers. One need never grow old so long as there are apples: "If you feel old age approaching you need only taste an apple to feel young again." So said Odin, the god of poetry.

And, indeed, it is the apple itself that seems to have eternal life, through numerous stories, legends, superstitions, and myths, and countless delicious recipes—the apple has been and will be the food for all time and all occasions.

Apples in North America

Apples have long been a part of our history. When the early European settlers came to North America, they brought along seeds and plants of their favourite vegetables, fruits, and flowers. Among them were apple seeds and seedlings, for planting in the New World.

Each pioneer family planted a variety of trees to ensure a fruit supply from August until the following spring. Orchards were usually planned in such a way as to have selective varieties, each ripening in successive rotation. On Prince Edward Island, for example, an orchard would possibly grow Yellow Transparent, Red Astrakhan, McIntosh, Cortland, Northern Spy, and Baxter varieties, with the first fruit ripening in August and the last in late fall, ready to be stored for winter. Apples were carefully picked by family members. The earliest apples would be eaten right off the trees, made into pies and sauces, and used quickly; later varieties were preserved, dried, or stored. Apples were first stored in piles on the clay floors of root cellars and covered in sand or straw, and later in wooden barrels. Apples were stored carefully, since there would be no other fresh fruit until rhubarb and strawberries came in the spring.

Many apples were also used in beverages, in the form of sweet cider, hard cider, or apple jack. As the following poem shows, it was a serious problem if the apple cider barrel was emptied too soon:

The Cider's Gittin' Low

When the farmer's stock of fodder he has placed within the barn,
When he's gathered all the apples and has placed them safe from Harm,
When the butchering is over, then the farmer feels so-so;
But he's always sort of worried, fer the cider's gittin' low.
He sees the signs of Winter in the breastbone of the fowl;
And he fears a spell of weather for he's heard a hooting owl.
As he fills the yawning woodbox, he remarks, "It's goin' to snow."
Then he says, "We must be careful, fer the cider's gittin' low."
When the cold and snapping breezes bend the sere and leafless trees,
When a pile of feathery snowflakes is the most a farmer sees,
Then he comes in from the tavern and he whispers rather slow,
"Goin' to be a freezin' winter and the cider's gittin' low."
So throughout the winter season and partway through the spring

The farmer feeds the cattle and doesn't say a thing;
But when he sees us drinking, with his face expressing woe,
He remarks, while helping mother, that "the cider's gittin' low."
(Author unknown)

Apple trees were growing in Port Royal, Nova Scotia, as early as 1609, planted there by the original French settlers. It takes a few years to establish an apple orchard, and the first record of apple harvesting in Canada is attributed to Pierre Martin of Annapolis Royal, Nova Scotia, around 1633. In the United States, the first apple tree was recorded to have been planted in 1629 by Governor Endecott of the Massachusetts Bay Colony, and about ten years later an orchard was set out in present-day Boston by William Blaxton, owner of the first Yellow Sweeting tree.

Some of the early North American settlers were from Normandy and Brittany, areas famous for apple cider. They were experienced apple growers and planted trees wherever they settled throughout the Maritimes, the eastern United States and, eventually, the coast of British Columbia. A census taken in 1698 recorded over 1,500 apple trees in the Annapolis Royal area of Nova Scotia alone. By the 1700s, fruit trees were one of the main resources of the Acadian people. When the Acadians were deported in 1755, they left behind well-established orchards, which were turned into commercial apple growing operations on a larger scale by the New England settlers who came to the Annapolis Valley in the 1760s.

It was the early 1800s before the cultivation of apples was organized in such a way as to grow selective varieties. Until then, apples had developed by seed and seedlings, and many varieties developed through chance matings. In fact, over seven thousand varieties of apple have developed in North America over the years, most by chance seedlings. In the United States, John Chapman—more popularly known as "Johnny Appleseed"—did much to cover the lands of the New World with early North American apple varieties. A lesser-known apple enthusiast, Charles Prescott, did much for the promotion of apples, and particularly Gravenstein apples, in the Canadian Maritimes. He experimented by testing varieties from other countries to see what was best for the Maritime climate. It is said that when he died in 1859, every farmer in Nova Scotia had at least one Gravenstein apple tree.

One truly Canadian apple is the McIntosh, which was developed in Dundas County, Ontario, around 1800. John McIntosh was a Scottish immigrant who found twenty apple trees on his land in Dundela, Ontario.

One of these trees was exceptional, and he began selling seedlings from it for grafting. The variety, which was called the McIntosh Red, did not become popular until nearly ninety years later when spraying techniques were developed to cut down on apple scab. In 1912, a marble monument was erected near what was believed to be the spot of the first McIntosh tree. The plaque on the monument reads: "The Original McIntosh Red Apple Tree stood about twenty rods north of this spot. It was one of a number of seedlings taken from the border of the clearings and transplanted by John McIntosh in the year 1796."

The Hudson's Bay Company had much to do with the growth of apples and orchards on the west coast of the United States. As a joke, a young woman placed the seeds from two apples into the pocket of a Hudson's Bay Company official, Captain Simpson, at a banquet in London. Simpson later gave the seeds to the company's gardener, who planted them in Fort Vancouver. These seeds flourished, and one tree that grew from these seeds is still flourishing near the Columbia River. It is identified by a marker, reading: "The oldest apple tree in the Pacific Northwest."

Around the time the McIntosh was being developed in Ontario, the first orchards were being established in the Okanagan Valley in British Columbia. The Red Delicious began to be grown in the 1890s, followed by the Golden Delicious in 1914. Today these three varieties, the McIntosh, the Red Delicious, and the Golden Delicious, are the most popular apples in Canada. They are followed in popularity by the Granny Smith, which is usually imported from South Africa or New Zealand.

By the 1930s, Nova Scotia apples dominated the Canadian market—almost half of Canada's crop, and 60 percent of apples for export, came from that province. Today, Nova Scotia ranks fourth among the other provinces.

Although apples grow in all provinces of Canada, there are five main apple-growing areas. Each region has its own specialties. New Brunswick grows Melba, McIntosh, and Cortland; Nova Scotia favours Gravenstein, Northern Spy, McIntosh, and Delicious; Quebec grows Melba, Lobo, McIntosh, and Cortland; Ontario supplies McIntosh, Red Delicious, Northern Spy, Empire, Golden Russet, and Idared; and British Columbia is famous for Red and Golden Delicious, McIntosh, Newton, Winesap, and Spartan.

In the United States, full-time apple cultivation was recognized as necessary around 1900, and the commercial orchard was born. Apples are grown widely in thirty-five states today, although the Oregon and Washington valleys are the best-known apple cultivation areas.

If you shop around, most of these varieties and an extensive list of others can be found in most parts of North America, either at roadside stands or from local growers. While researching this book, I found over twenty varieties on Prince Edward Island alone—not to mention the many wild trees, with unamed varieties, that I've found and sampled with great results.

Apple Varieties

There are thousands of apple varieties in the world today. Because of poor keeping and shipping qualities, however, most varieties are grown only for local markets and in home orchards. Some of the varieties available throughout most of North America are the following:

Cortland—a large, flat-shaped, bright red, striped apple, suitable for snacks, salads, fruit cups, sauces, and baking. A general all-purpose apple.

Empire—a medium-sized, globular apple with dark red stripes and noticeable spots. Suitable for eating fresh and cooking.

Golden Delicious—an elongated apple, narrowing to a five-point base. It is a bright sunshine-yellow colour with a sweet, juicy, crisp flesh. One of the most universally available varieties, suitable for eating fresh and in all types of cooking.

Golden Russet—an apple grown for export in Europe. It actually came to Canada from England in the nineteenth century. The Golden Russet is a rusty-yellow, medium-sized, fragrant-smelling apple. An excellent eating apple that is available in late fall and throughout the winter months.

Granny Smith—an apple that originated in Australia and is grown primarily in Argentina, Africa, and New Zealand. It takes 190 days to mature, and must have a warm climate. A Granny keeps for up to seven months in normal refrigeration, and its tart, crispy texture is excellent for snacks and all culinary purposes.

Gravenstein—a popular variety in Nova Scotia. Medium-sized, globular in shape, with red stripes on a greenish-yellow background. It is uncertain where the Gravenstein originated. One theory states it was grown in the Castle Graefenstein in Schleswig-Holstein in the early 1800s. Another idea postulates that it came from Italy to Gråsten Castle in Jutland. It is a rather difficult apple to grow, as it ripens over a long period. It is best cooked into pies and sauces. The flavour turns bland about a month after picking, so Gravensteins should be used quickly.

Idared—a large, deep-red apple with greenish-yellow patches, developed in Idaho in 1942. The flavour mellows with storage. Idared is an excellent apple for eating, cooking, and processing.

McIntosh—one of the most popular and best-tasting apples. It was developed in 1796 in Dundela, Ontario. A medium-sized, irregular, globe-shaped apple, deep red in colour with green splashes. It is mildly acid with a juicy, very white flesh and rather tough skin. It cooks soft and smooth and is excellent for sauces, eating fresh, and processing, but is not suitable for baking whole as it does not hold its shape. McIntosh apples are abundant in fall, and usually available most of the year.

Newton—an apple unsurpassed for every use. Medium-sized, irregular, and globe-shaped, green in colour, with yellow or blush shading. The Newton is excellent for eating, cooking, and processing, and is a good keeper. It has a tangy flavour and crisp pulp, and stays firm when cooked.

Northern Spy—one of the later varieties. The Spy was developed in Rochester, New York, in the 1840s. It is a large, bright red apple with yellowish flesh. Moderately tart, it is ideal for freezing and holds its shape well when baked. Suitable for cooking, commercial processing, snacks, salads, and baking. One of the finest all-purpose varieties.

Red Delicious—thought to be the best-known apple in the world. It was first developed in Iowa in 1874. An elongated apple, narrowing to a five-point base, bright red in colour with a sweet, juicy, crisp flesh. The skins are a bit tough. Red Delicious loses its shape when cooked, but is excellent for eating fresh, in snacks, salads, and fruit cups. Red Delicious is also used for processing.

Rome Beauty—a large, round apple, red striped, with pin dots. Has a very mild, bland flavour that is fair for eating but best when baked or cooked. A Rome Beauty keeps its shape, but needs spices for flavour when cooked.

Spartan—a medium-to-large, globular apple, solid red with white pin dots. A very attractive apple that is excellent for eating fresh and also quite good for most cooking uses. The Spartan stores well for three to four months in cold storage.

Winesap—a medium-sized, globular apple, deep red in colour with yellow splashes and white pin dots. A late-season apple, and an excellent keeper. The Winesap has a mildly tart, wine-type taste. It is a firm apple suitable for snacks, salads, baking whole, and all culinary uses, as well as processing.

Yellow Transparent—an apple imported from Russia in 1870. Usually the first early apple on the market, the Yellow Transparent is small to medium in size and greenish yellow in colour. It has a sweet, rather bland taste and is a watery apple that bruises easily and should be used within a week of picking. The Yellow Transparent is seldom found in stores; instead, it is usually available at roadside stands or farmers' markets.

Of the above varieties, Red and Golden Delicious, Granny Smith, and McIntosh are available virtually all year round, and are the four most popular apples in North America.

Some apples are all-purpose, while others are best for a specific use. Generally speaking, tart apples are best for cooking and preserving, while low-acid apples are best for eating and salads. Late varieties have more fibre and hold their shape better for baking.

Golden Delicious and Cortland stay white longer than other varieties, and so are excellent for salads and fruit cups. When using other varieties in a salad, dip them in a solution of lemon juice and water or an ascorbic-acid mixture to prevent darkening. Apples used for eating should have a crisp, juicy, firm texture. Apples that are good for pies are also good for stewing, frying, dumplings, and apple crisps.

Be adventuresome with your apples. Try different varieties and combinations to find your favourites.

Harvesting

There are three basic rules to follow when picking apples: never shake an apple tree, never pull on the fruit, and pick one apple at a time. The proper technique for picking apples, called the rolling method, is as follows:

• An apple should be held lightly between the palm of the hand and the thumb and forefinger. It should be removed from the tree by gently turning it with a lifting motion until it is upside down on the spur. If the fruit is ready to pick, it will separate easily, without damaging the spur or disturbing other fruit. Pulling apples from the tree causes the branches to shake loose other fruit, which fall and bruise. Pulling can also remove fruit buds and thus reduce next year's crop.

• Handle apples gently, and leave on stems to prevent infection from bacteria in the air. Be careful not to drop apples—set them gently in your container. Bruising is the major cause of apple cullage.

• Pick apples from the lower limbs first—if one happens to drop while picking the higher limbs, it won't damage other fruit as it falls. If you are picking apples commercially, be sure to dress for the job: wear layers of clothing; avoid sweaters that can snag in tree limbs; wear comfortable work boots and heavy socks, preferably with a change for midday. Clothing that can be changed and layered throughout the day is the only suitable choice for apple picking.

Buying and Storing

When buying fruit, it is always wise to buy the ones in season. Buy only what you will use in a reasonably short period of time.

Reject damaged fruit unless you have an immediate use for it. Handle fruits carefully and never squeeze them, as they bruise easily. Handle apples even more carefully than you would eggs—apples bruise much more easily than an egg will break. Don't get carried away with size, as the biggest apple is not always the best.

Store your apples away from other fruits and vegetables to prevent odours transferring from one to another. Choose firm, ripe apples that have been picked properly. Avoid apples that are bruised or have the stems removed. Cool apples as soon as possible and do not wash them before storing. Store in baskets, or cardboard or wooden containers, and store only a few layers deep. Check periodically, and remove any overripe apples or any that are beginning to spoil.

If you buy a small bag of apples at the grocer's, store them in your refrigerator crisper in the perforated bag in which they came. Never leave your apples at room temperature—they ripen quickly at room temperature and soon will be soft and unappetizing.

Controlled Atmosphere (CA) Storage

In the 1950s, controlled atmosphere storage came into practice, combining an airtight refrigeration of 32 degrees Fahrenheit, or 0 degrees Celsius, with an atmosphere of reduced oxygen and increased carbon dioxide. Lack of oxygen slows down the ripening process, greatly extending the life of an apple. Apples stored in controlled atmosphere look like perfectly ripened apples. However, they may taste a bit overripe if they have been stored for long periods.

Apples that are marketed over a shorter period of time are stored under refrigeration at temperatures just above freezing.

Nutritional Information

Fruit is a valuable source of fibre, vitamins, and minerals and an important addition to our daily diet. For centuries, people have enjoyed the beauty, aroma, flavour, and texture of apples. They are not, in fact, an excellent source of any one nutrient, but contain a variety of essential minerals and vitamins. Because they have few calories as well, apples are a popular part of our diet and have come to have more culinary uses than any other fruit.

In addition to containing vitamins and minerals, apples are about twelve percent fructose, a water-soluble sugar found in all ripe fruit. Because of the solubility of fructose, the body does not have to convert it into sugar before use, therefore making apples a source of instant energy.

Apples are high in pectin, a soluble fibre that can absorb more water than any other bulking agent; fibre, in turn, is linked to a lower incidence of colon cancer, hemorrhoids, coronary heart disease, dental cavities, and obesity, and helps the body in the absorption of cholesterol into the bloodstream. Lower cholesterol helps reduce heart disease.

Fresh fruit helps in weight control. As well as being low in calories, the fibre and pectin found in apples slow the rate at which the stomach is emptied, thus prolonging a satisfied, full feeling and reducing the desire to eat more food. The apple is also suited to low-sodium diets.

Apples are a "detergent" food because they work to clean the digestive system, and act as nature's toothbrush. Eating an apple cleans the teeth and massages the gums, removing more bacteria than two three-minute brushings followed by a gargle.

A three-and-a-half-ounce apple can be broken down as follows:

Water: 84.4%

Calories: 58

Protein: 0.2 grams

Fat: 0.6 grams

Carbohydrates: 14.5 grams

Fibre: 1 gram

Ash: 0.3 grams

Calcium: 7 milligrams

Phosphorus: 10 milligrams

Iron: 0.3 milligrams

Sodium: 1 milligram

Potassium: 110 milligrams

Vitamin A: 90 IU

Thiamine: 0.03 IU

Riboflavin: 0.02 IU

Niacin: 0.1 IU

Vitamin C (Ascorbic Acid): 4 milligrams

Scientists have proven that apple eaters have fewer headaches, intestinal disorders, colds, respiratory problems, and illnesses associated with the nervous system.

You can eat an apple with complete peace of mind: it tastes good, adds fibre to your diet, and won't rot your teeth.

Apple Products

Apple juice is the natural juice of apples which has been filtered several times and pasteurized to a clear, bland liquid. Apple juice is sold in cans and jars as well as in a frozen concentrate.

Apple jelly is made from a combination of apple juice and sugar. Pectin is added to some apple jellies, depending on the tartness of the apples. Some producers also add corn syrup and citric acid.

Apple butter is a concentrated mixture of apples, sugar, and spices.

Apple pie filling is made from pared, cored, sliced, sweetened, and flavoured apples that have been thickened with starch. Apple pie filling comes in both cans and jars.

Applesauce is made from one variety or a combination of several apples. It can be made by cooking peeled, cored, and thinly sliced apples in a small amount of water and sweetening to taste. Or it can be made by cooking unpeeled apples and putting the cooked mixture through a food mill. To prepare the apples, the blossom and stem ends are removed and apples quartered before cooking.

Apple cider is apple juice that has been filtered fewer times than pasteurized juice. It may be brownish in colour and may look cloudy. Cider is sometimes pasteurized and may have soda added to delay fermentation. Fresh cider will keep refrigerated for a week. Pasteurized cider and apple juices should be refrigerated after opening. Fresh cider freezes well.

"Hard" apple cider is fermented cider—it usually contains about 7 percent alcohol. Hard cider can be distilled into apple brandy called "applejack."

Apple brandy or calvados is fermented cider that is heated, vaporized, and condensed back into liquid form. Freezing apple brandy removes water and leaves behind applejack.

Dried apples are apple rings or pieces of peeled, cored apples that have most of the moisture removed.

Frozen apples are now available and are usually packaged in peeled, cored slices suitable for pie-making.

Apple Cider

Thanks to Dennis Hopping of Gaylden Orchard, Mills Point, PEI, for contributing this information.

The art of making apple cider has been part of the orchard industry in North America for hundreds of years. It apparently evolved from the European immigrants who came to the Americas and planted some of the original orchards.

Apple cider is the puréed apple juice from apples that have been crushed in a press. Methods of making apple cider vary from small, hand-operated machines to large commercial operations capable of pressing many hundreds of pounds of cider at one time.

In all cases, the apples are first ground in a grinder that reduces them to small chunks or chips. These chips are then placed in light canvas bags or cloths similar to cheesecloth, and stacked or piled into the press. Placing the ground apples in bags or cloths allows only the juice to be extracted from the apple pulp, thereby keeping most of the ground apple pieces out of the cider once pressing commences. The press applies pressure to the bags and squeezes them until all the juice has been extracted. Once this process has been completed, the pulp is taken from the press bags and discarded. It can be used as animal feed (for cattle, sheep, or pigs) or composted for use in gardens and flowerpots.

The juice must be kept refrigerated to ensure that the natural fruit yeast contained in the apples does not start to ferment. This action will turn the cider into wine or "hard cider"—a product that contains varying percentages of alcohol.

Cider can vary in taste from very tart to very sweet. In order to obtain an attractive colour and moderately sweet product, most cider producers use a number of apple varieties while pressing. One of the most popular apple mixtures includes McIntosh, Spartan, Cortland, and Paula Red.

APPETIZERS
AND BEVERAGES

Appetizers, served before a meal, stimulate the digestive juices and whet the appetite for the meal to come.

Preparation of party nibblers is often the most time-consuming part of entertaining. Not so with these tasty tidbits. Whether you're preparing Apple & Bacon Bites, Mary's Mini Meatballs, or any of the recipes found in this section, these excellent eatables will save you time and delight your family and friends.

Beverages are a staple part of every meal and social gathering. Always keep a supply of teas, coffees, fruit juices, and mixes on hand for an endless supply of tasty drinks that take minutes to prepare. Preparing beverages can be the most trouble-free form of the culinary art. There are two simple rules to follow: be sure your ingredients are the proper temperature and never over-sweeten drinks. As well, preparing fruit juice in ice cube trays for punch bowls will keep your punch cold without diluting the taste.

AVOCADO APPETIZERS

Avocados filled with mixed fruit and a tangy mint dressing.

1 cup mandarin orange
   segments, drained

1 large red apple, cored,
   quartered, and sliced

1 large banana, peeled
   and sliced

3 tbsp vegetable oil

3 tbsp lemon juice

1 tbsp granulated sugar

1 tsp fresh mint

1/4 tsp salt

3 medium avocados, halved
   and pits removed

mint sprigs for garnish,
   if desired

Combine orange segments, apple slices, and banana slices in a bowl. Add lemon juice, sugar, and salt to vegetable oil; mix well. Pour 2 tbsp of this mixture over the fruit and mix lightly. Set avocado halves on serving plates. Brush hollow of each half with the extra salad dressing. Fill with fruit mixture. Garnish with mint sprigs. Serve with remaining dressing.

APPLE & BACON BITES

Little one-bite treats that will have you going back for more.

slices of white bread,
   crust removed and cut
   in bite-sized pieces

mayonnaise

bacon, fried until crisp
   and cut in 1 1/2-inch
   pieces

apples, cored, quartered,
   and thinly sliced

lemon juice, optional

Dip apple slices in lemon juice, if desired. Place bread in a 325°F oven and bake for about 10 minutes, to toast lightly. Spread with mayonnaise, cover with 2 slices of apple, and top with a piece of bacon. Serve at once.

APPLE SANDWICHES

Easy appetizers for a children's party. Children can even help make them.

apple, washed, cored, and
  sliced crosswise

fruit juice, lemon, orange,
  or pineapple

peanut butter

cream cheese

Dip apple rings in fruit juice. Spread 1 ring with peanut butter or cream cheese, top with another ring. Cut into thirds or quarters, depending on the size of the apple.

MARY'S MINI MEATBALLS

A sweet-and-sour glaze tops these moist miniatures.

MEATBALLS:

1 lb lean ground beef

2 medium apples, pared,
  cored, and grated

1/4 tsp ginger

1 tbsp soya sauce

1 egg

2–3 tbsp vegetable oil

GLAZE:

1/2 cup cider vinegar

1/2 cup granulated sugar

4 tsp soya sauce

Meatballs: Combine beef, apples, ginger, soya sauce, and egg. Mix well and shape into small balls. Pour vegetable oil into a large frying pan. Fry meatballs over medium heat until browned. Turn often. Be sure not to overcrowd the pan, or turning the meatballs will be difficult. Drain meatballs and keep warm while preparing the glaze.

Glaze: Combine glaze ingredients in a small saucepan. Bring to a boil and cook until thickened. Pour over warm meatballs and toss lightly to coat. Serve immediately.

Variation: Use ground pork instead of beef for an equally delicious appetizer.

COCKTAIL MEATBALLS

This recipe from the kitchen of Virginia Parker of Orlando, Florida, is sure to be a favourite. I seldom use prepared mixes in cooking, but make an exception in this case. This is one of my family's favourite dishes for a potluck supper.

2 lbs ground meat
(beef, pork, venison,
or a mixture)

1 envelope onion
soup mix

1 egg

1/2 cup fine bread
crumbs

1 tbsp butter

1 1/4 cups apple jelly

3 cups ketchup

Combine meat, onion soup mix, egg, and bread crumbs. Form into small meatballs. Brown in butter over medium heat. Set aside for about 30 minutes to firm. Mix apple jelly and ketchup. Bring to a simmer and add meatballs. Simmer gently until heated throughout.

FRUITED MOCHA FOAM

Thank you, Nova Scotia Growers Association, for this different and delicious apple drink.

2 apples, peeled, cored,
and diced

1 ripe banana, cut in
chunks

2 tsp instant coffee

2 tbsp instant cocoa

3 tbsp granulated sugar

2/3 cup non-fat dry milk

1 2/3 cups ice water

1 tsp vanilla

Combine all ingredients in an electric blender. Operate on low speed until fruit is liquified. Beat on high speed until foamy. Serve. Makes 2 or 3 servings.

APPLE SNACKLE

Makes a great instant breakfast.

1 egg

3/4 cup chilled apple
  juice

1/3 cup cold milk

1 tsp honey

1/4 tsp cinnamon

sprinkle of nutmeg, if
  desired

Combine all ingredients; beat until frothy.
Pour into a tall glass, and garnish with a
sprinkling of nutmeg if desired. Serve at
once. Makes 1 portion.

APPLE QUENCHER

Ireland is the home of this yummy drink.

1/2 cup natural yogurt

pinch of cinnamon or
  cloves

1/2 cup apple juice

Combine all ingredients in a blender and
whirl until smooth. Serve immediately.
Makes 1 portion.

CHRISTMAS WASSAIL

Through the centuries, it's been a Christmas tradition in many countries to "Wassail,"or drink to the health of others, during the festive season. What better way than with a hot, spiced apple drink!

8 cups apple juice

4 cups pineapple juice

1 cup lemon juice

2 cups orange juice

1 tsp whole cloves

1 stick cinnamon

granulated sugar to taste

Combine all ingredients in a pot or large kettle. Bring to a simmer. Check for sweetness. Simmer about 10 minutes to blend flavours. Serve hot. Serves 20 to 24.

"APPLE A DAY" MILKSHAKE

Your child will love this homemade milkshake. The recipe makes just enough to share with a friend.

1 cup cold milk

1 large scoop vanilla ice cream

2 tbsp frozen apple juice concentrate

1/2 apple, pared, cored, and chopped

cinnamon, optional

Combine ingredients in an electric blender; cover and blend until smooth. Sprinkle with cinnamon, if desired.

EARL GREY APPLE DAPPLE

A delightful thirst quencher that blends two of my favourite drinks, apple juice and Earl Grey tea. Iced tea with a difference.

6 Earl Grey tea bags (regular tea may be used)

3 cups boiling water

4 cups apple juice

2 tbsp lemon juice

granulated sugar to taste

ice cubes

lemon slices for garnish, if desired

Put tea bags in a heated teapot. Pour over freshly boiling water. Let steep 5 minutes. Pour into an iced-tea pitcher. Let stand at room temperature until cool. Stir in apple and lemon juice. Sweeten to taste. To serve, pour over ice cubes. Garnish with lemon slices, if desired. Serves 6 to 8.

APPLE TEA

2 apples, cored and thinly sliced

rind and juice of 1 lemon

1 tbsp honey (optional)

3 cups rapidly boiling water

Place apples, honey, and lemon juice in a pot. Pour boiling water over. Cover and let stand for 5 minutes. Strain and serve. Serves 4.

CONNIE'S HOT MULLED CIDER

A wintertime favourite from the kitchen of Connie Marchbank of Wilmot, Prince Edward Island.

8 cups apple juice

1/2 cup brown sugar

1 tsp whole allspice

1 tsp whole cloves

1/4 tsp salt

dash of ground nutmeg

1 (3-inch) cinnamon stick

Combine all ingredients in a covered saucepan. Bring slowly to a boil and simmer for 20 minutes. Strain before serving. Serves 8 to 10.

Alternate Preparation Method:
Place juice and sugar in the base of an automatic coffee maker; put spices in the basket. Let run through the "perk" cycle.

MID-WINTER HOT PUNCH

8 cups apple juice

3 cups cranberry juice

4 sticks cinnamon

1 tsp whole cloves

2 1/2 cups vodka

lemon slices and cinnamon sticks for garnish, if desired

Heat apple juice, cranberry juice, cinnamon, and cloves to boiling point. Simmer 5 minutes to blend flavours. Remove spices, cool slightly. Add vodka. Serve warm. Makes 20 servings.

APPLE-CRANBERRY PUNCH

16 cups sweet apple cider

10 cups cranberry juice

6 1/2 cups ginger ale

1 orange, thinly sliced

Combine apple cider and cranberry juice. Chill thoroughly. Just before using, pour mixture into punch bowl. Add ginger ale, lemon juice, and orange slices. Makes 30 servings.

Note: Apple juice may be used in place of cider, if desired.

ISLAND WEDDING PUNCH

12 cups water

2 cups granulated sugar

3 tea bags
(orange pekoe)

2 cups water

3 cups (2 small cans)
frozen lemon juice,
thawed slightly

3 cups (2 small cans)
frozen orange juice,
thawed slightly

8 cups cranberry juice,
chilled

4 cups apple juice, chilled

4 cups ginger ale, chilled

Combine 12 cups water and 2 cups sugar in a large saucepan. Bring to a boil. Cool thoroughly and chill in refrigerator. Bring the 2 cups water to boil and add tea bags. Let steep 10 minutes. Remove tea bags, cool, and chill tea. Just before serving, combine water/sugar mixture with tea and juices. Stir to blend. Pour into punch bowl; add ginger ale and serve immediately.

Note: Water frozen in a 2-cup salad mould makes a nice ice cube for this punch.

BREAKFASTS

Nutritionists tell us breakfast is the most important meal of the day, yet many of us skip breakfast or settle for juice and coffee and a slice of toast. The recipes in this section will tempt you to change that habit. During those laid-back mornings, treat yourself to High Rise Apple Pancakes or Apple & Bacon Quiche. If time is scarce, try Hot Apple Oatmeal or Apple Eye-Opener, each of which can be prepared in minutes. Start your day right with a healthy, tasty breakfast—you'll be surprised how much better your day will be.

APPLE-BUTTERMILK PANCAKES

I like to serve these with maple syrup and sausages.

1 cup all-purpose flour

1 tbsp granulated sugar

1/2 tsp baking powder

1/2 tsp salt

1/2 tsp baking soda

1 cup buttermilk

1 beaten egg

2 tbsp butter, melted

1 cup apples, peeled, cored, and grated

Combine flour, sugar, baking powder, and salt. Stir baking soda into buttermilk. Add to flour mixture along with egg and butter. Stir only until blended. Fold in apples. Bake on a very lightly greased griddle. When batter is full of bubbles, turn over to brown on other side. Pancakes are best if turned only once during cooking.

Note: To test for proper temperature for cooking pancakes, drop a few drops of water on hot griddle. If the water dances, the pan is the right temperature. For an electric griddle, set temperature to 350 to 375°F.

MOM'S APPLE PANCAKES

I've been eating these pancakes for nearly half a century and I still think they're the best.

1 1/2 cups all-purpose flour

3 tsp baking powder

1/2 tsp salt

3 tbsp granulated sugar

1/4 tsp nutmeg

1/3 tsp baking soda, dissolved in 1 tsp water

1 egg

3 tbsp butter, melted

1/4 tsp vanilla

1 cup milk

1 cup apples, peeled and grated

Combine flour, baking powder, salt, sugar, and nutmeg. In a separate dish, mix baking soda, egg, butter, vanilla, and milk. Combine both mixtures, stirring only until blended. Fold in grated apple. Bake on a hot, lightly greased griddle. When batter is full of holes, turn over to brown on other side. Turn pancakes only once while cooking.

HIGH RISE APPLE PANCAKES

From the kitchen of my sister, Cheryl Hessel, of Vancouver Island.

4 tbsp butter or margarine

6 cups apples, peeled, cored, and sliced

3–4 tbsp granulated sugar (depending on sweetness of apples)

1/2 tsp cinnamon

2 eggs, slightly beaten

1/2 cup all-purpose flour

1/2 cup milk

1/4 tsp salt

1 tbsp butter or margarine

strawberry or apple jam

Melt butter in a large skillet, over low heat. Add apples, sugar, and cinnamon. Cook until apples are tender. Preheat oven to 450°F. Combine eggs, flour, milk, and salt. Beat until smooth. Heat an ovenproof skillet in the oven until very hot. Coat skillet with butter or margarine and immediately pour in batter. Bake on the lowest rack of the oven for 10 minutes. Reduce heat to 350°F. Continue cooking until golden brown, about 10 minutes. Fill pancake with apple mixture and top with strawberry jam. Serve immediately.

APPLE-SIDE UP

The Canadian Egg Marketing Agency gives us this delicious instant breakfast for one.

1 egg

3/4 cup apple juice, chilled

1/4 cup cold milk

1 tsp honey

1/4 tsp cinnamon

Combine all ingredients in a blender. Blend until frothy. Serve at once.

APPLE POPOVERS

3 medium apples, peeled, cored, and halved

1 tbsp margarine, melted

1/4 cup brown sugar

shake of cinnamon, optional

1 1/2 cups all-purpose flour

1/2 tsp salt

1/2 cup lard

3–4 tbsp cold water

Mix apples with margarine and sugar. Sprinkle with cinnamon, if desired. Set aside. Preheat oven to 425°F. Combine flour and salt. Cut in lard and add enough water to make a fairly stiff pastry. Roll pastry into thin rectangle. Cut out squares of pastry to cover apple halves. Place apple halves on pastry squares and fill cavities with sugar mixture. Fold over pastry and seal, making a 3-sided turnover. Prick pastry with fork in several places. Bake until pastry is browned and apples are tender, approximately 20 minutes. Cooking time will vary slightly with the size and firmness of the apples.

HOT APPLE OATMEAL

Porridge with a difference, from BC Fruits.

4 1/2 cups apple juice

2 cups rolled oats

1 cup apples, peeled, cored, and diced

1/2 cup raisins

1/4 tsp salt

1/2 tsp cinnamon

Combine all ingredients in a saucepan. Bring just to boiling, lower heat, and simmer, stirring occasionally, for 5 minutes, until oatmeal is as thick as you like it.

APPLE-CRANBERRY CRÊPES

CRÊPES:

1/3 cup all-purpose flour

2 tbsp granulated sugar

1/2 tsp salt

2 eggs

2/3 cup milk

1 tbsp butter, melted

1 tsp vanilla

FILLING:

1/4 cup butter

2 cups apples, peeled, cored, and sliced

1 cup cranberries, coarsely chopped

1/4 cup brown sugar

1 tsp cinnamon

2 tsp lemon juice

Crêpes: In a small bowl, stir together flour, sugar, and salt. In a separate bowl, beat eggs, and stir in milk, melted butter, and vanilla. Add to dry ingredients and beat well. Lightly grease a 7- or 8-inch skillet and heat over medium heat. Pour about 2 tbsp batter into hot pan. Tilt pan to spread batter. Cook about 1 minute on each side. Repeat until all batter is used. Stack crêpes with waxed paper between them.

Filling: Preheat oven to 350°F. Melt butter in skillet over medium heat. Add apple slices, cranberries, sugar, cinnamon, and lemon juice. Cook gently until apples are tender, about 10 minutes. Spoon about 1/4 to 1/3 cup filling over each crêpe.

Roll crêpes and arrange in a baking pan. Bake for about 15 minutes, until heated through. Serve hot with whipped cream or ice cream.

BC APPLE-SAUSAGE BRUNCH

1 lb sausages

2 large onions, sliced

2 large apples, cored and cut into rings

parsley for garnish

Brown sausages in large skillet until cooked through. Drain all but 1 tbsp fat. Add onions and sauté until tender. Stir in apple rings and sausages. Cook about 5 minutes until apples are tender. Garnish with parsley, if desired.

APPLE-HAM BRUNCH PUFF

Apples and ham topped with a golden puffed pancake make a delicious holiday brunch.

4 medium, tart apples, peeled, cored, and sliced

3 cups cooked ham, diced

3–4 tbsp brown sugar

shake of pepper

1/4 tsp mace

1/4 cup apple juice

1 cup pancake mix

1 cup milk

2 tbsp melted butter

Preheat oven to 350°F. Spread a layer, consisting of half the apples and half the ham, in the bottom of a 2-quart baking dish. Combine sugar, pepper, and mace and sprinkle half the mixture over apples and ham. Cover with remaining apples and ham and sprinkle with rest of sugar mixture. Pour apple juice over top. Bake until apples are tender, about 45 minutes.

Combine pancake mix, milk, and butter. Pour over hot apple-ham mixture. Return to oven and bake until topping is golden brown.

APPLE SCRAMBLE

Eggs and apples are a nutritious and delicious combination for breakfast or brunch. The Nova Scotia Department of Agriculture suggests this lovely combination.

2 tbsp vegetable oil

1 medium onion, chopped

1/2 cup red or green pepper, chopped

1 garlic clove, minced

1 large apple, cored and thinly sliced

4 eggs

2 tbsp apple juice

1/2 tsp nutmeg

pinch of pepper

1/2 cup cheddar cheese, grated

Heat oil in a medium-size skillet. Add onion, chopped peppers, and garlic, and cook over low heat until the onion is tender. Add apple and cook for a few minutes longer. Beat eggs with apple juice, nutmeg, and pinch of pepper. Pour egg mixture into skillet and sprinkle with cheese. Stir and cook until eggs are set and cheese is melted. Serve at once with crispy toast.

APPLE EYE-OPENER

I clipped this recipe from a magazine a few years ago when I had a teenager who never had time for breakfast. It's perfect for a growing teenager.

1 apple, peeled, cored, and sliced

1 cup milk

2 tbsp peanut butter

1/4 tsp vanilla

Combine all ingredients in a blender and whirl for 2 minutes. Serve at once.

BROWN BETTY BREAKFAST

Apples and creamy brown rice make a delicious high-fibre cereal.

1 1/2 cups cooked brown rice

2 cups milk

2 tbsp sugar or honey

1/4 cup raisins

2 eggs, slightly beaten

1 cup apples, peeled, cored, and chopped

1/2 tsp vanilla

2 tsp butter

1/2 tsp nutmeg

Combine rice, milk, sugar, and raisins in top of a double boiler. Cook over simmering water until heated through. Stir in beaten eggs. Cook until mixture thickens. Stir in apples, vanilla, and butter. Spoon into serving dishes and sprinkle with nutmeg. Serve at once.

Note: Add a bit of hot mixture to eggs before stirring beaten eggs and mixture together. This prevents the eggs from cooking before being properly mixed in.

APPLE & BACON QUICHE

This recipe from BC Tree Fruits Limited isn't just for breakfast. It's perfect any time.

pastry for 9-inch pie pan

5 strips side bacon

1/4 cup onion, diced

1 cup apples, peeled and thinly sliced

1 cup (4 ounces) Swiss cheese, grated

3 eggs

1/2 tsp salt

1/4 tsp dry mustard

2/3 cup (1 small can) evaporated skim milk

Preheat oven to 425°F. Press pastry into pie pan. Bake for 5 minutes. Reduce oven heat to 375°F. In a large skillet, fry bacon until crisp. Drain all bacon fat, except 1 tbsp. Sauté onion and apple until tender, about 5 minutes. Crumble bacon, and place in pie shell with onion and apple. Sprinkle with grated cheese. In medium mixing bowl, combine eggs, salt, mustard, and milk. Mix well with a wire whisk. Pour into pie shell. Bake 15 minutes. Let stand 15 minutes before serving.

BREADS

Bread making has changed greatly since the days when it was buried in hot sand and cooked around the wagon trains. Today, making bread is so easy that even the novice cook can have perfect results with a first attempt. If you've never baked yeast bread before, read the hints for making better bread in this chapter. Pick the recipe of your choice and simply follow the directions. There's something special about hot biscuits with jam, or yeast breads with creamy butter. Slices of delicious quick breads will make your well-deserved coffee break even more pleasant.

All recipes (except fritters) in this chapter can be frozen for up to six months to give you a supply of anytime breads. Cool bread completely, and wrap in foil or put in plastic freezer bags. Be sure to take as much air as possible out of the freezer bags. (I find a plastic drinking straw is good for this.) To serve, unwrap and thaw at room temperature.

For lunch boxes, snacks, or an accompaniment to any meal, there's nothing better than bread.

Hints for Making Better Bread

The water used to dissolve yeast should be about 105°F. To test the temperature, put a drop of water on the inside of your wrist. It should feel warm, but not hot. Water that is too hot will kill the yeast action.

With the first addition of flour, beat the batter well to ensure that all ingredients are blended.

To knead dough, fold toward you, and then push away with the heel of your hand. Rotate dough a quarter-turn and repeat until dough is smooth and surface looks blistered. A good way to tell if dough has been kneaded enough is to pinch the dough with one hand while squeezing your ear lobe with the other hand. They should feel about the same.

Cover dough and set to rise in a warm, draft-free place.

To test for double bulk, stick fingertips into dough; the marks should remain if dough has doubled.

To punch down, shut your fist and plunge it into the centre of the dough.

Bake breads with the top of the pan level with the middle of the oven. Be sure pans have space all the way around them and are not touching the sides of the oven.

You can tell that bread is done when you tap the crust and it sounds hollow. To test quick breads, insert cake tester or toothpick into centre of loaf. If it's done, the tester or toothpick should come out clean; the bread should also be leaving the sides of the pan. One other method of testing is to press the centre of the bread with your finger—if the loaf is done, the indentation should pop back up as soon as the finger is removed.

Remove bread from pans and place on wire racks to cool. Cool away from drafts.

Store bread in a tightly covered breadbox at room temperature, or wrap in foil or plastic wrap and put in your freezer. Bread dries out quickly if kept in the refrigerator.

APPLE-BANANA BREAD

1/2 cup shortening	1/2 cup applesauce
3/4 cup granulated sugar	2 cups all-purpose flour
2 eggs, well beaten	1 tsp salt
3 tbsp sour milk	1 tsp baking soda
1/2 cup mashed banana	

Preheat oven to 350°F. Grease and line 9 x 5-inch loaf pan. Cream shortening and sugar until fluffy. Add eggs, sour milk, banana, and applesauce; mix well. Sift flour, salt, and baking soda; add to mixture. Mix until thoroughly blended. Pour into prepared pan. Bake approximately 50 minutes.

APPLE-CINNAMON BREAD

Apple, cinnamon, fruit, and nuts make this loaf an anytime favourite.

2 1/4 cups whole wheat flour	1/2 cup applesauce
2 tsp baking powder	1/2 cup molasses
1 tsp cinnamon	1/4 cup margarine, melted
1/2 tsp baking soda	1/4 tsp almond extract
1/4 tsp salt	1 egg
2 cups apples, coarsely grated	1/2 cup walnuts, chopped

Preheat oven to 350°F. Grease 8 x 4-inch loaf pan. In a large bowl, combine flour, baking powder, cinnamon, baking soda, and salt. Stir until well blended. In a separate bowl, combine apple, applesauce, molasses, margarine, almond extract, and egg. Add liquid ingredients to dry ingredients and mix thoroughly.

Stir in walnuts. Pour into prepared pan and bake 1 hour. Cool on a wire rack.

FLO'S APPLE BREAD

This quick and easy recipe from the kitchen of Florence Hopkins of Fairview, Nova Scotia, is sure to be a favourite.

2 cups all-purpose flour

1 tsp salt

1 tsp baking soda

1 1/2 tsp baking powder

1/2 cup granulated sugar

1/2 tsp cinnamon

1/4 tsp mace

2 eggs, beaten

1/4 cup shortening, melted

1 tsp vanilla

1/4 cup apple juice

1 cup apples, grated

1/4 cup walnuts, chopped

Preheat oven to 350°F. Grease 9 x 5-inch loaf pan; line bottom with waxed paper. Sift together flour, salt, baking soda, baking powder, sugar, cinnamon, and mace. Combine eggs, shortening, vanilla, and apple juice. Add to dry mixture. Mix well. Stir in walnuts. Pour into prepared pan. Bake 50 to 60 minutes.

APPLE-CHEESE LOAF

2 eggs, lightly beaten

2/3 cup sugar

1/2 cup vegetable oil

1 1/2 cups apple, unpeeled and grated

1/2 cup cheddar cheese, grated

2 cups all-purpose flour

1 1/2 tsp baking powder

1/2 tsp baking soda

1/2 tsp salt

1/2 cup walnuts, chopped (optional)

Preheat oven to 350°F. Lightly grease 9 x 5-inch loaf pan. In a large mixing bowl, add sugar to eggs and beat well. Pour in vegetable oil, and mix. Add apples and cheese. Stir in flour, baking powder, baking soda, and salt. Stir briskly until all ingredients are combined. Fold in nuts. Pour into prepared pan and bake 50 to 60 minutes. Remove from pan and cool on wire rack.

APPLE-BRAN LOAF BREAD

This delicious and nutritious yeast loaf has only 92 calories a slice and is suitable for most diabetic diets.

3 cups apples, pared, cored, and sliced

1 cup apple juice

3 cups bran

3 tsp salt

3/4 cup granulated sugar

3 tbsp butter, melted

2 1/4 cups boiling water

1 1/2 tsp granulated sugar

3/4 cup warm water

3 tbsp yeast

12 cups all-purpose flour

Simmer apples and apple juice for 5 minutes. Pour into a blender and whirl until smooth. Cool to lukewarm. Combine bran, salt, sugar, butter, and boiling water. Cool to lukewarm. Meanwhile, dissolve 1 1/2 tsp sugar in warm water and sprinkle with yeast. Let sit 10 minutes.

Combine yeast and apple mixture in a large bowl. Add half the flour and beat well. Stir in remaining flour and knead until it forms a smooth dough. Let rise until double in bulk, about 1 1/2 hours. Punch down. Form into 3 loaves. Put in greased loaf pans and let rise for 1 hour.

Preheat oven to 350°F. Bake for 1 hour or until loaves sound hollow when tapped on the bottom. Remove from pans and cool on wire rack.

CELEBRATION BREAD

I've been unable to find the origin of this unusually named recipe, but the apples and cranberries in this loaf are a combination that is a celebration in itself.

3/4 cup shortening

1 cup brown sugar, firmly packed

3 large eggs

2 tsp vanilla

3 cups all-purpose flour

1 1/2 tsp salt

1 1/2 tsp baking soda

1 1/2 tsp cinnamon

3/4 tsp nutmeg

1/2 tsp cloves

1 1/2 cups apples, pared and finely grated

3 tbsp lemon juice

2/3 cup water

1 cup cranberries, chopped

3/4 cup pecans, chopped

Preheat oven to 350°F. Grease 2 (8 x 4-inch) loaf pans. Cream shortening and sugar. Add eggs one at a time; beat well after each addition. Stir in vanilla. Sift flour, salt, baking soda, cinnamon, nutmeg, and cloves. Add to flour mixture alternately with apples, lemon juice, and water. Mix well. Fold in cranberries and pecans. Pour into prepared pans. Bake for 1 to 1 1/4 hours, until tests indicate that the bread is done. Remove from pan and cool on wire racks.

APPLE QUICK BREAD

1/2 cup shortening

1 cup granulated sugar

2 eggs, beaten

1 tsp vanilla

2 cups all-purpose flour

1/4 tsp salt

1 tsp baking soda

1 tsp baking powder

1 cup apples, peeled, cored, and finely chopped

1 1/2 tbsp sour milk

Preheat oven to 325°F. Grease and flour 8 x 4-inch loaf pan. Cream shortening and sugar. Beat in eggs and vanilla. Sift flour, salt, baking soda, and baking powder. Add to egg and sugar mixture along with apples and sour milk. Mix until thoroughly moistened. Do not overmix. Spread in prepared pan and bake 1 hour.

APPLE & CARROT QUICK BREAD

Every fall, it seems, there are some damaged carrots when I take in my garden. Finely grated, they can be used in a variety of loaves, cakes, and puddings that will keep at least three months in your freezer. I like to make several of these loaves each fall, when carrots and apples are abundant.

1/2 cup granulated sugar

1/3 cup salad oil

1 egg

1/2 cup whole wheat flour

1/2 cup all-purpose flour

3/4 tsp baking soda

1/2 tsp salt

1 tsp cinnamon

1 cup carrots, grated

1 cup apples, grated

1/2 cup raisins

Preheat oven to 350°F. Grease 8 x 4-inch loaf pan. Blend sugar, oil, and egg. Sift flours, baking soda, salt, and cinnamon. Add to liquid ingredients along with carrots, apples, and raisins. Pour into prepared pan. Bake for 1 hour.

Note: I use a very large mixing bowl and multiply the ingredients by 4 when I make this loaf. 4 loaves will cook nicely in most modern ovens.

APPLESAUCE-BRAN BREAD

1/4 cup shortening

1/2 cup granulated sugar

1 large egg, beaten

1 cup bran cereal flakes, slightly crushed

1 1/2 cups all-purpose flour

2 tsp baking powder

1/2 tsp salt

1/2 tsp baking soda

1 tsp cinnamon

1/2 tsp cloves

1 cup chopped nuts

1 cup applesauce

Preheat oven to 350°F. Grease and flour 9 x 5-inch loaf pan. Cream shortening and sugar. Add egg and beat well. Stir in cereal. Sift flour, baking powder, salt, baking soda, cinnamon, and cloves; add nuts. Add flour mixture and applesauce alternately to first mixture. Mix thoroughly. Spoon into prepared pan and bake for 1 hour. Cool overnight before cutting.

APPLESAUCE & BLUEBERRY BREAD

We're lucky to have August apples and blueberries coming on the market at the same time. My family has been known to serve this bread hot from the oven, with ice cream, a whipped topping, or a brown sugar sauce.

1/4 cup butter, melted

1 cup granulated sugar

2 eggs, well beaten

1 cup applesauce

3 cups all-purpose f lour

3 tsp baking powder

1 tsp salt

1/2 tsp baking soda

1/2 tsp mace

2 cups blueberries

Preheat oven to 350°F. Grease 2 (8 x 4-inch) loaf pans. Cream butter and sugar. Beat in eggs. Add applesauce. Sift flour, baking powder, salt, baking soda, and mace. Sprinkle about 1/2 cup flour mixture over blueberries. Toss to coat. Add remaining flour mixture to batter. Mix thoroughly. Stir in blueberries. Pour batter into prepared pans. Bake 45 to 50 minutes. Cool 5 minutes in pan before removing to a wire rack.

APPLESAUCE-PUMPKIN TEA BREAD

This recipe makes two loaves. They freeze well.

2/3 cup salad oil

2 cups granulated sugar

1/3 cup molasses

3 eggs, beaten

1 cup applesauce

1 cup mashed pumpkin

1/3 cup milk

3 2/3 cups all-purpose flour

1 1/2 tsp baking powder

2 tsp baking soda

2 tsp cinnamon

1 tsp nutmeg

1 tsp vanilla

1 cup raisins

1 cup walnuts, chopped

Preheat oven to 350°F. Spray 2 (8 x 4-inch) loaf pans with non-stick cooking spray. Combine salad oil and sugar; mix well. Add molasses, eggs, applesauce, pumpkin, and milk. Beat until well blended. In a separate bowl, combine flour, baking powder, baking soda, cinnamon, and nutmeg. Stir to mix thoroughly. Add to liquid mixture, along with vanilla. Stir in raisins and nuts, and mix thoroughly. Pour into prepared pans. Bake for 1 hour. Cool on a wire rack.

APPLESAUCE-OATMEAL TEA BREAD

1 egg, well beaten

3/4 cup brown sugar

2 cups all-purpose flour

4 tsp baking powder

1/2 tsp salt

1 tsp cinnamon

1/2 tsp nutmeg

3/4 cup applesauce

1/2 cup water

2 tbsp vegetable oil

1 cup rolled oats

Preheat oven to 350°F. Grease a 9 x 5-inch loaf pan.

Add brown sugar to beaten egg and blend well. Sift together flour, baking powder, salt, cinnamon, and nutmeg. Add to egg mixture along with applesauce and water. Mix well. Stir in vegetable oil and rolled oats. Pour into prepared pan and bake for 1 hour. Remove from pan and cool on a wire rack.

Note: For variation, add 1/2 cup raisins or chopped dates.

ENGLISH APPLE TEA BREAD

This recipe from England is a favourite when served at afternoon tea. I think it's lovely anytime.

TEA BREAD:

5 cooking apples, peeled, cored, and sliced

1/2 cup fine granulated sugar

1 tbsp water

1/3 cup plus 1 tbsp sunflower or vegetable oil

1/2 cup milk

2 large eggs

1 cup all-purpose flour

1 cup whole wheat flour

1 1/2 baking powder

1/2 tsp salt

1/3 cup sultana raisins

TOPPING:

2 medium dessert apples

1 tbsp granulated sugar

GLAZE:

reserved apple juice

1 tbsp pistachio nuts, or pecans

Tea Bread: Combine cooking apples, sugar, and water in a saucepan. Cool over low heat for 15 minutes, until mixture is soft. Pour into a sieve or strainer and drain, reserving juice. Cool completely. Preheat oven to 350°F. Grease and line the bottom of an 8 x 4-inch loaf pan. In a large mixing bowl, beat together oil, milk, and eggs. Sift flours, baking powder, and salt. Add to egg mixture along with raisins and drained apples. Mix well. Put in prepared pan and smooth top of batter.

Topping: Arrange apple slices over batter. Sprinkle with sugar and bake for 1 to 1 1/2 hours, until cake tester comes out clean. Cool in tin for 15 minutes before removing to a wire rack to cool completely.

Glaze: Pour reserved apple juice into a small saucepan. Bring to a boil, and boil rapidly until juice is reduced in volume and has the consistency of a heavy syrup. Brush over apple slices to glaze. Sprinkle with chopped nuts.

APPLE TEA BISCUITS

Serve these biscuits warm, with butter and honey or apple marmalade.

4 cups all-purpose flour

1/2 cup granulated sugar

4 tsp baking powder

1 tsp baking soda

1 tsp salt

1/2 cup margarine

2 cups apples, pared, cored, and grated

1 cup milk

Preheat oven to 425°F. Combine flour, sugar, baking powder, baking soda, and salt. Cut in margarine until crumbly. Add apple and milk, and stir with a fork until dough holds together. Knead gently to form a smooth ball. Pat dough to 1-inch thickness. Cut with biscuit cutter and place on greased baking sheet. Bake for 15 minutes, until biscuits are golden brown on top and light in weight. Serve warm.

Variation: Currants, raisins, or mixed fruit may be added to biscuit batter. You can also brush tops with milk or egg white and sprinkle with cinnamon and sugar for an added touch.

MELT-IN-YOUR-MOUTH MUFFINS

This recipe yields 18 muffins chock full of chunks of apple. McIntosh are the recommended apples to use.

2 cups all-purpose flour

1/4 cup granulated sugar

1/2 tsp salt

1 tbsp baking powder

1/2 tsp cinnamon

1/4 tsp mace

1/4 cup butter, melted

1 cup milk

1 egg, lightly beaten

1 cup apples, pared and grated

1/2 cup raisins

Preheat oven to 400°F. Prepare 18 muffin cups. Sift flour, sugar, salt, baking powder, cinnamon, and mace. Combine butter, milk, and egg; add to dry ingredients. Stir until thoroughly moistened. Add apples and raisins. Spoon into muffin cups. Bake for 18 to 20 minutes.

SPICY BC APPLE BUNS

These delicious buns from a BC Tree Fruits Limited recipe are guaranteed to quickly disappear. I like to make these buns each December 24 and serve them for breakfast on Christmas morning.

1 tbsp yeast

1 tsp granulated sugar

1/4 cup warm water

TOPPING:

1 1/2 cups apples, peeled and diced (Spartan are recommended)

1/2 cup raisins

1/4 tsp cloves

1/4 tsp nutmeg

1/2 tsp cinnamon

2 tbsp flour

1/4 cup brown sugar

DOUGH:

1 cup butter

2 1/2 cups all-purpose flour

3 eggs, beaten slightly

1 tbsp butter, melted

GLAZE:

1 cup icing sugar

2 tbsp apple juice

GARNISH:

Red and green maraschino cherries (optional)

Dissolve yeast and sugar in warm water. Set aside.

Topping: In medium bowl, toss topping ingredients together.

Dough: To make dough, cut butter into flour to form even crumbs. Add eggs and yeast mixture. Beat to form a smooth ball, 3 to 5 minutes. On a well-floured surface, knead dough lightly until no longer sticky. Roll dough into a 15 x 12-inch rectangle. Sprinkle melted butter over the surface. Spread topping over dough. Start with longer side and roll up lightly, sealing the edges. Cut into 17 rolls. On a greased cookie sheet, arrange slices to form a Christmas tree; the top of the tree is 1 roll, the next row 2 rolls, the next 3, and so on. Use 2 rolls for the tree trunk. Cover, and let rise in warm place until light and doubled in size, 30 to 45 minutes.

Glaze & Garnish: Preheat oven to 350°F and bake 20 to 30 minutes, until golden brown. Cool, then glaze with mixture of icing sugar and apple juice. Garnish with red and green maraschino cherries for a more festive look, if desired.

SPICED APPLE MUFFINS

From the kitchen of Shirley Matheson of Wilmot, PEI, these muffins are mouth-watering.

MUFFINS:

1/3 cup vegetable oil

1 cup milk

1 egg

1 cup apples, pared, cored, and finely chopped

2 cups all-purpose flour

1/2 cup granulated sugar

3 1/2 tsp baking powder

1/2 tsp salt

TOPPING:

2 tbsp brown sugar

1/4 tsp nutmeg

1/4 tsp cinnamon

Muffins: Preheat oven to 400°F. Combine oil, milk, and egg. Beat lightly. Mix in apples. Combine dry ingredients, and toss to mix. Stir dry ingredients into liquid mixture, until thoroughly blended. Spoon into greased or lined muffin cups, filling each cup 2/3 full.

Topping: Combine brown sugar, nutmeg, and cinnamon. Sprinkle over muffins. Bake for 15 to 20 minutes.

Note: I use a small-sized ice cream scoop for filling muffin cups with batter. The muffins will be uniform in size, and there are no spots of batter dropping from your spoons onto pans or workspace.

APPLE CHELSEA BUNS

A lovely "sticky" bun from across the sea. In England, recipes for Chelsea buns have been passed down through the centuries. I'm glad this particular recipe found its way to Canada.

2 cups applesauce

1 cup brown sugar

1 tsp cinnamon

1/2 cup pecans, chopped

1/2 cup sultana raisins

1 1/4 cups milk

1 tsp granulated sugar

1/4 cup warm water

1 tbsp yeast

5 cups all-purpose flour, approximately

1 1/2 tsp salt

1 cup granulated sugar

1/2 cup shortening

2 large eggs

1/4 cup butter

2 cups corn syrup, divided

Combine applesauce, brown sugar, and cinnamon in a small saucepan. Cook over low heat until thickened. Remove from heat, stir in pecans and raisins, and cool. In another small pan, scald milk and let cool to lukewarm. Meanwhile, dissolve 1 tsp granulated sugar in water. Sprinkle with yeast and let stand 10 minutes.

In a large bowl, combine yeast and milk. Add 2 cups flour, salt, and 2 tbsp sugar. Beat until smooth. Set in a warm place to rise until double in bulk.

Beat remaining sugar and shortening until fluffy. Add eggs one at a time, beating well after each addition. Add shortening mixture to risen yeast mixture, along with remaining flour. You should have a soft dough. Cover and let rise for 1 hour or until doubled. Grease 24 large muffin cups. Put 1 scant tbsp corn syrup in the bottom of each cup.

Divide dough into two equal portions. Roll each portion into a thin rectangle. Spread with half butter and half apple mixture. Roll as you would for jelly roll, beginning with the long side of rectangle. Cut each roll into 12 pieces. Put 1 piece into each muffin cup. Cover and let rise for 30 to 35 minutes. Preheat oven to 350°F. Bake buns for 30 minutes. Remove from pans at once. Serve hot.

Note: These buns are a nice treat to serve after a skating party or sleigh ride. They take about 3 hours to make and are best served hot. The recipe can be halved, but there's never any problem polishing off the full 2 dozen buns.

WHOLE WHEAT APPLE-CARROT MUFFINS

1 cup whole wheat flour

1/4 cup granulated sugar

1/4 cup dry skim milk powder

1 1/2 tsp baking powder

1/2 tsp cinnamon

1/4 tsp salt

1/4 tsp nutmeg

1/2 cup oil

1/2 cup liquid honey

2 eggs

1/2 tsp vanilla

1/2 cup apples, pared and grated

1/2 cup carrots, pared and grated

Preheat oven to 400°F. Grease 12 muffin cups or line with paper liners. Combine flour, sugar, milk powder, baking powder, cinnamon, salt, and nutmeg in a mixing bowl. In a separate bowl, combine oil, honey, eggs, and vanilla. Beat lightly with a wire whisk until blended. Add grated apple and carrot to liquid mixture. Stir well. Fold in dry ingredients, mixing with a spoon until thoroughly moistened. Do not overmix. Fill muffin cups 2/3 full. Bake for 20 to 25 minutes.

APPLESAUCE-OATMEAL MUFFINS

One dozen tasty muffins from the kitchens at Cackleberry Farms, Prince Edward Island.

3/4 cup all-purpose flour

1/2 tsp cinnamon

1/2 tsp nutmeg

1/2 tsp salt

1 tbsp baking powder

1 1/4 cups rolled oats

3/4 cup raisins

1/2 cup vegetable oil

1/2 cup brown sugar

1 large egg

1 cup applesauce

Preheat oven to 400°F. Grease or line 12 muffin cups. In a large bowl, combine flour, cinnamon, nutmeg, salt, baking powder, rolled oats, and raisins. Toss to mix. In a separate bowl, mix oil, sugar, egg, and applesauce. Whisk lightly until well blended. Stir in flour mixture. Divide between muffin cups. Bake for 20 minutes.

AUTUMN APPLE MUFFINS

I often make these muffins for my mother-in-law, who has diabetes. One muffin has 114 calories and equals 1 starch choice, 1/2 fruit choice, and 1/2 fat choice. An altogether top recipe from BC Fruit Trees Limited.

1 egg, slightly beaten

2 tbsp soft butter

1/4 cup granulated sugar

1/4 cup plain yogurt

1/3 cup milk

1/2 cup bran

1 medium apple, pared and grated (preferably McIntosh)

1/2 cup raisins (soaked a few minutes in hot water and drained)

1/2 cup rolled oats

1/3 cup whole wheat flour

1/3 cup all-purpose flour

3/4 tsp baking powder

1/2 tsp baking soda

3/4 tsp cinnamon

1/4 tsp salt

Preheat oven to 425°F. Grease 12 muffin cups. In a large bowl, combine egg, butter, sugar, yogurt, milk, bran, apple, raisins, and rolled oats. Sift together flours, baking powder, baking soda, cinnamon, and salt. Combine both mixtures and stir only until moistened. Spoon into muffin cups. Bake for 25 minutes.

Note: Mix muffins only until moistened. Overmixing will cause tough muffins.

APPLE STRUDEL MUFFINS

Possibly the quickest muffins ever—you don't even have to peel the apples.

MUFFINS:

2 cups all-purpose flour

1 cup granulated sugar

3 tsp baking powder

1 tsp cinnamon

1/2 tsp salt

1/2 tsp baking soda

2 large eggs, beaten

1 cup sour cream

1/4 cup butter or margarine, melted

1 cup apples, finely diced

STRUDEL TOPPING:

1/4 cup granulated sugar

3 tbsp all-purpose flour

1/2 tsp cinnamon

2 tbsp butter

Muffins: Preheat oven to 400°F. Grease or line 18 muffin cups. Combine flour, sugar, baking powder, cinnamon, salt, and baking soda in a large mixing bowl. In a smaller bowl, mix beaten eggs, sour cream, and melted butter or margarine. Add to dry ingredients and stir only until moistened. Lightly fold in apples. Fill prepared muffin cups 2/3 full.

Topping: Combine granulated sugar, flour, cinnamon, and butter. Mix with a fork until crumbly. Sprinkle over muffins. Bake 20 to 25 minutes.

APPLE 'LASSIES MUFFINS

One of my favourite snacks is bread and molasses...maybe that's why I like these muffins. There's nothing quite like molasses and spice for flavour.

1/2 cup butter or margarine

1/2 cup brown sugar

3/4 cup molasses

2 large eggs

1/3 cup milk

2 cups all-purpose flour

3 tsp baking powder

2 tsp cinnamon

1 tsp salt

1 tsp allspice

2 cups apples, pared and finely diced

1/2 cup walnuts, chopped

Preheat oven to 375°F. Grease or line 18 large muffin cups. Combine butter, sugar, molasses, and eggs. Beat until well blended. Add milk. Sift together flour, baking powder, cinnamon, salt, and allspice. Add all at once to creamed mixture. Mix until well moistened. Stir in apples and walnuts. Divide into muffin cups, filling about 3/4 full. Bake for 25 to 30 minutes. Cool 10 minutes and serve warm.

APPLE-CARROT MUFFINS

A nutritious breakfast or bedtime snack.

2 cups all-purpose flour

3 tsp baking powder

2 tsp cinnamon

1 tsp baking soda

1/2 tsp salt

4 eggs

1 cup granulated sugar

1/4 cup vegetable oil

1/4 cup milk

2 tsp vanilla

1 cup carrots, peeled and finely grated

1 cup apples, pared and finely grated

1/2 cup walnuts, optional

Preheat oven to 375°F. Grease 12 large muffin cups or line with paper liners. Combine flour, baking powder, cinnamon, baking soda, and salt in a large mixing bowl. In a separate bowl, beat eggs; add sugar, oil, milk, vanilla, carrot, and apple. Stir to blend. Stir in dry ingredients and walnuts. Mix only until thoroughly moistened. Fill muffin cups 2/3 full. Bake for 20 to 25 minutes.

APPLE DATE-NUT MUFFINS

Serve these hot with plenty of butter and apple jelly.

MUFFINS:

2 cups all-purpose flour

1/2 cup granulated sugar

1 tbsp baking powder

1/2 tsp salt

1/4 tsp nutmeg

1 egg

1 cup milk

1/3 cup butter, melted

1 tsp vanilla

3/4 cup apples, pared
   and finely grated

1/2 cup dates, finely
   chopped

TOPPING:

2 tbsp granulated sugar

1 tsp cinnamon

1/4 tsp cloves

1/4 tsp mace

Muffins: Preheat oven to 375°F. Grease or line 12 large muffin cups. Sift flour, sugar, baking powder, salt, and nutmeg into a large mixing bowl. In a separate bowl, beat egg, milk, butter, and vanilla. Combine the two mixtures. Stir to blend. Add apples, walnuts, and dates. Do not overmix. Fill muffin tins 2/3 full.

Topping: Combine sugar, cinnamon, cloves, and mace. Sprinkle over muffins. Bake for 25 to 30 minutes.

APFELSTRUDEL (APPLE STRUDEL)

There are many versions of apple strudel from Austria, Hungary, Germany, and Czechoslovakia. This recipe is my own version, adapted from several recipes I found while researching this book.

STRUDEL PASTRY:

1 1/2 cups all-purpose flour

1/2 cup lukewarm water

2 tbsp vegetable oil

1/2 tsp salt

2 tbsp butter, melted

STRUDEL:

6 cups apples, pared, cored, and chopped

2 tbsp lemon juice

1/4 cup butter, melted

1/4 cup fine, very dry breadcrumbs

1 cup granulated sugar

1/4 cup walnuts, finely chopped

1/2 cup sultana raisins

1 tsp cinnamon

Strudel Pastry: Combine flour, water, vegetable oil, and salt. Mix well until flour is thoroughly moistened and dough clings together. Knead on a lightly floured surface until dough is smooth and no longer sticky. Use the minimum of flour in kneading. Shape into a ball, brush with melted butter, and let rest for about 1/2 hour. Meanwhile, prepare to make strudel.

Strudel: Preheat oven to 375°F. Toss apples in lemon juice. Set aside.

Cover a large workspace with a tablecloth. Pin cloth tightly (I use masking tape for this). Sprinkle cloth with flour. Roll dough to 1/8-inch thickness. Place hands, palms down and close together, under dough. Gently lift and stretch until dough is paper thin and covers an area about 2 1/2 to 3 feet square.

Brush square with melted butter and sprinkle breadcrumbs down one side of square in a 3-inch strip about 2 inches in from edge of dough. Combine sugar, walnuts, raisins, cinnamon, and apple mixture. Spread in a 3-inch strip over breadcrumbs. Lift edge of cloth and roll like a jelly roll, lifting cloth as you roll dough. Place on a greased cookie sheet, seam side down, in a circular or U-shaped position, or cut in centre to make 2 rolls. Seal all ends. Brush with melted margarine. Bake 35 to 45 minutes. Remove from oven and sprinkle with icing sugar.

QUICK APPLE STRUDEL

2 cups all-purpose flour

3 tsp baking powder

1/2 tsp salt

2 tbsp granulated sugar

1/4 cup shortening

3/4 cup milk

2 tbsp butter, melted

3 cups apples, peeled,
cored, and chopped

1/2 cup granulated sugar

1 tsp cinnamon

icing sugar

hot water

lemon or vanilla extract

chopped walnuts or
pecans

Preheat oven to 425°F. Grease a cookie sheet. Sift flour, baking powder, salt, and 2 tbsp sugar. Cut in shortening until mixture resembles fine crumbs. Add milk to make a soft dough. Turn out onto a floured surface and roll to 1/4-inch thick. Brush with melted butter, cover with chopped apples, and sprinkle on 1/2 cup sugar and cinnamon. Roll in a jelly roll fashion. Place roll of dough in a semi-circular pattern on prepared cookie sheet. Bake for 20 to 30 minutes. Meanwhile, mix icing sugar with a little warm water and flavour to taste with lemon or vanilla extract. While strudel is warm, drizzle with icing sugar mixture. Sprinkle with chopped nuts.

COOKIES

I remember our small daughter reciting a verse that went something like this:

Some Grammas drive in limousines
And live in houses just like queens,
But my Gramma's best by far
Because she's got a cookie jar.

I've no idea who wrote these words, but I'm sure all children agree there's something special about Gramma's cookie jar. This chapter features recipes from many "grammas" who enjoy making cookies, myself included. No special ingredients are needed and the recipes are easy to prepare, so let your little ones help. Many of my fondest memories centre around cookie making with my gramma, my mom, my children, and now my grandson. Your sweet tooth will give you all the encouragement you need to begin trying these cookies of all kinds.

APPLE-WALNUT COOKIES

2 cups all-purpose flour

1 cup rolled oats

1 1/2 tsp baking soda

3/4 cup shortening

1 1/2 cups brown sugar

3/4 tsp salt

1 1/2 tsp cinnamon

1 tsp cloves

1/4 tsp nutmeg

2 eggs

1/3 cup apple juice

1 1/2 tsp walnuts, ground fine

1 1/2 cups apples, unpeeled and finely chopped

1 1/2 cups raisins

Preheat oven to 400°F. Combine flour, rolled oats, and baking soda. In another bowl, mix shortening, sugar, salt, cinnamon, cloves, nutmeg, and eggs. Beat well. Add flour–rolled oat mixture alternately with apple juice. Stir in walnuts, apples, and raisins. Drop on greased cookie sheet and bake 10 to 12 minutes.

Note: When baking cookies, be sure to put pans on the middle rack of your oven. Baking on the bottom rack may result in "burnt offerings."

CHOCOLATE CHIP APPLE COOKIES

The Nova Scotia Fruit Growers Association offers this recipe for moist and delicious cookies.

1/2 cup butter

1/2 cup granulated sugar

1/2 cup brown sugar

1 egg

3/4 cup whole wheat flour

3/4 cup all-purpose flour

1/2 tsp salt

1/2 tsp baking soda

1/2 tsp ginger

1 cup apples, pared and grated

3/4 cup chocolate chips

1/2 cup rolled oats

Preheat oven to 350°F. In a large bowl, cream butter and sugars; beat in egg. Mix flours, salt, baking soda, and ginger; stir into creamed mixture. Stir in grated apple, chocolate chips, and rolled oats. Drop mixture by rounded teaspoons onto well-greased baking sheet. Bake for 15 minutes or until golden brown. Yields approximately 30 cookies.

APPLE-GRANOLA COOKIES

1/2 cup butter

1/2 cup granulated sugar

1/2 cup brown sugar

1 egg

3/4 cup whole wheat flour

3/4 cup all-purpose flour

1/2 tsp salt

1/2 tsp baking soda

1 tsp cinnamon

1/4 tsp cloves

1/4 tsp allspice

1 cup apples, pared and grated

1/2 cup granola

1/2 cup rolled oats

1/2 cup raisins

Preheat oven to 350°F. Cream butter and sugars; add egg, and mix well. Combine flours, salt, baking soda, cinnamon, cloves, and allspice. Add to creamed mixture. Stir in grated apple, granola, rolled oats, and raisins. Drop by teaspoons on a well-greased cookie sheet. Bake for 15 minutes or until golden brown.

APPLE SPICE COOKIES

This recipe makes a large batch of cookies, but don't be scared to double the ingredients. They will disappear quickly. From the kitchen of Lorraine Peters of Summerside, PEI.

1 cup shortening

2 1/2 cups granulated sugar

1 1/2 tsp cinnamon

1 tsp cloves

1 tsp ginger

1/2 tsp nutmeg

2 tsp salt

2 tbsp baking soda

1 cup dark molasses

1/2 cup milk

4 1/2 cups all-purpose flour

extra sugar

apple jelly

Preheat oven to 350°F. Cream shortening and sugar until fluffy. Stir in cinnamon, cloves, ginger, nutmeg, salt, and baking soda. Add molasses and milk alternately with flour. Mix well. Roll dough into walnut-sized balls. Toss dough balls in granulated sugar. Place on lightly greased cookie sheets. Indent centres of cookies with your finger and fill indentations with apple jelly. Bake 12 minutes.

APPLESAUCE COOKIES

1 cup seedless raisins

1/2 cup boiling water

3 1/4 cups all-purpose flour

1 tsp baking soda

1 tsp salt

1 tsp cinnamon

1/4 tsp nutmeg

1/4 tsp cloves

1 cup butter

3/4 cup granulated sugar

3/4 cup brown sugar

2 eggs

1/2 cup unsweetened applesauce

1/2 cup walnuts, chopped (optional)

Preheat oven to 350°F. Pour boiling water over raisins; let sit a few minutes, then drain well. Discard water. Sift flour, baking soda, salt, cinnamon, nutmeg, and cloves. In a separate bowl, cream butter and sugars until fluffy. Add eggs one at a time, beating well after each addition. Stir in dry ingredients, applesauce, raisins, and nuts. Mix well. Drop in rounded teaspoons onto a well-greased cookie sheet. Bake for 12 to 15 minutes.

APPLESAUCE-CURRANT COOKIES

This recipe comes from the kitchen of our lovely daughter-in-law, Stacey.

1/2 cup butter or margarine

1 cup brown sugar, firmly packed

1 large egg

1 tsp vanilla

2 cups all-purpose flour

1 tsp baking powder

1/2 tsp baking soda

1/2 tsp salt

1 tsp pumpkin pie spice

1 cup applesauce

1 cup currants

Cream butter and sugar until fluffy; beat in egg and vanilla. Sift flour, baking powder, baking soda, salt, and spice; add alternately with applesauce. Stir in currants. Drop by rounded tablespoons onto well-greased cookie sheets. Leave 5 inches between cookies, as they spread into 2 1/2- to 3-inch rounds. Bake for 15 minutes, until browned around the edges. Cool on wire racks. Leave plain or sprinkle with icing sugar. This recipe yields about 2 dozen large cookies.

APPLESAUCE TROPICAL TREATS

The combination of applesauce, pineapple, and coconut gives these cookies a tropical flavour.

1 cup butter or margarine

1 1/4 cups granulated sugar

2 eggs

1 tsp vanilla

1 tsp lemon juice

2 1/2 cups all-purpose flour

1 1/2 tsp baking powder

1/2 tsp salt

1/2 cup applesauce

1/2 cup crushed pineapple

1 cup shredded coconut

Cream butter and sugar until light and fluffy. Beat in eggs, vanilla, and lemon juice. Sift flour, baking powder, and salt; add to creamed mixture alternately with applesauce and pineapple. Stir in coconut. Cover batter and chill in refrigerator until firm.

Preheat oven to 325°F. Drop rounded teaspoonfuls of dough on greased cookie sheets, leaving about 2 inches between cookies. Bake for 15 minutes. Cool on wire racks.

APPLESAUCE-MOLASSES DROP COOKIES

1 cup butter or margarine

2 1/2 cups granulated sugar

4 eggs

2/3 cup molasses

3 1/2 cups all-purpose flour

2 tsp baking powder

2 tsp cinnamon

1/2 tsp salt

1 cup applesauce

4 cups rolled oats

2 cups raisins

1 cup walnuts, chopped

Preheat oven to 375°F. Cream butter and sugar until fluffy. Beat in eggs and molasses. Sift flour, baking powder, cinnamon, and salt; add alternately with applesauce. Stir in rolled oats, raisins, and walnuts. Drop by rounded teaspoonfuls on greased cookie sheet. Bake 15 to 18 minutes.

OATMEAL-APPLESAUCE DROP COOKIES

These are not only delicious cookies, but nutritious as well.

3/4 cup shortening

1 cup brown sugar, firmly
    packed

1 egg

1 cup applesauce

1/2 cup raisins

2 cups all-purpose flour

1/2 tsp baking soda

1/2 tsp salt

1/2 tsp cinnamon

1/2 cup milk

Preheat oven to 400°F. Cream together shortening and brown sugar. Beat in egg. Add applesauce and raisins. Sift flour, baking soda, salt, and cinnamon. Add to creamed mixture alternately with milk. Mix until smooth. Drop by rounded teaspoonfuls on greased cookie sheets. Bake approximately 15 minutes.

MINCEMEAT COOKIES

A favourite of my husband, this recipe features homemade Apple-Tomato Mincemeat. If you haven't got homemade mincemeat on hand, the canned varieties work well, but will have a stronger flavour.

3/4 cup margarine

3/4 cup granulated sugar

3/4 cup brown sugar

2 eggs

1 tsp vanilla

2 tsp rum flavouring

2 1/2 cups all-purpose flour

1 tsp baking powder

1/2 tsp baking soda

1/2 tsp salt

1/2 tsp cinnamon

1/2 tsp nutmeg

1/4 tsp cloves

1 1/2 cups Apple-Tomato Mincemeat (see page 201 for recipe)

Preheat oven to 350°F. Cream margarine and sugars until fluffy. Add eggs one at a time, and beat well after each addition. Blend in vanilla and rum flavouring. Sift flour, baking powder, baking soda, salt, cinnamon, nutmeg, and cloves: stir into creamed ingredients alternately with mincemeat. If necessary, add an extra bit of all-purpose flour to make a fairly stiff dough. Drop by rounded teaspoonfuls onto lightly greased cookie sheets. Leave plenty of room for spreading. Bake 15 to 20 minutes. Cool on wire racks.

CHRISTMAS APPLE HERMITS

The idea for these cookies came one year when I was wondering how to use bits of fruit and nuts leftover from my Christmas baking. These cookies keep well and make nice last-minute Christmas gifts. To make them extra fancy, try a rum and butter icing and top with a walnut or pecan half.

2/3 cup butter

1 cup brown sugar, firmly packed

2 eggs

1/4 cup honey

2 cups all-purpose flour

1 1/2 tsp baking powder

3/4 tsp cinnamon

1/2 tsp mace

1/2 tsp salt

1/2 tsp baking soda

1/4 tsp allspice

1/4 tsp cloves

1/4 tsp ginger

1 cup unsweetened applesauce

1 cup seeded raisins, chopped

1/2 cup mixed fruit

1/4 cup walnuts, chopped

Preheat oven to 375°F. Cream butter and sugar until fluffy. Add eggs one at a time and beat well. Stir in honey. Sift flour, baking powder, cinnamon, mace, salt, baking soda, allspice, cloves, and ginger. Add alternately to creamed mixture along with applesauce. Mix until well blended. Stir in raisins, fruit, and nuts. Drop by teaspoonfuls onto greased cookie sheets, leaving about 2 inches between cookies. Bake 15 to 18 minutes, until browned on the bottom and springy on top. Cool on wire rack.

These cookies are best after maturing for a day or two.

PEANUT BUTTER & JELLY COOKIES

An always popular cookie with children, featuring two favourites, peanut butter and apple jelly.

1 cup butter

1 cup peanut butter

1 cup granulated sugar

1 cup brown sugar

2 eggs

1 1/2 tsp vanilla

2 tbsp milk

4 cups all-purpose flour

2 tsp baking soda

1/4 tsp salt

1 cup flaked coconut
  (optional)

1/2 cup apple jelly

Preheat oven to 375°F. Cream butter, peanut butter, and sugars until light and fluffy. Beat in eggs, vanilla, and milk. Combine flour, baking soda, and salt. Stir into creamed mixture. Add coconut if desired. If dough is too sticky to handle, add a bit more flour or chill in refrigerator. Form dough into small balls using a rounded teaspoonful for each cookie. Put on an ungreased cookie sheet. Push a hole in the top of each cookie with the tip of your finger. Fill holes with about 1/2 tsp apple jelly. Bake 12 to 15 minutes.

APPLE-PECAN DROP COOKIES

COOKIES:

1/2 cup shortening

1 1/2 cups brown sugar

1 large egg

2 cups all-purpose flour

1 tsp baking soda

1 tsp salt

1 tsp cinnamon

1/4 tsp cloves

1/4 cup milk

2 cups apples, pared, cored, and finely grated

1 cup pecans, chopped

GLAZE:

1 cup icing sugar

1/2 tsp vanilla

1 tbsp melted butter

1 1/2 tbsp hot milk

Cookies: Preheat oven to 400°F. Cream shortening and sugar. Beat in egg. Sift flour, baking soda, salt, cinnamon, and cloves. Stir about half the dry ingredients into creamed mixture. Add milk, apples, and pecans. Stir in remaining dry ingredients. Mix well. Drop by teaspoonfuls onto greased cookie sheet. Bake 10 to 12 minutes.

Glaze: Mix all ingredients together. Spread glaze over cookies while still a bit warm. Cool completely on wire rack before storing.

APPLESAUCE-RAISIN COOKIES

These cookies freeze well. For special occasions, top with confectioner's icing and nuts or cherries.

1 cup butter or margarine at room temperature

3/4 cup granulated sugar

3/4 cup brown sugar

2 large eggs, slightly beaten

1 cup raisins

1 cup boiling water (poured over the raisins, then drained and discarded)

1/3 cup chopped nuts

3 1/2 cups all-purpose flour

1 tsp baking soda

1 tsp salt

1 tsp cinnamon

1/4 tsp cloves

1/4 tsp nutmeg

Preheat oven to 375°F. Cream butter and sugars. Add eggs and beat well. Pour boiling water over raisins, let stand a few minutes; drain, discarding water. Stir raisins and nuts into creamed mixture. Sift flour, baking soda, salt, cinnamon, cloves, and nutmeg. Add to batter and mix well. Shape dough in walnut-sized balls. Place on an ungreased cookie sheet. Flatten with a fork. Bake for 12 minutes. Cool on wire rack.

CATHY'S CHRISTMAS COOKIES

1 cup butter or margarine

1 cup granulated sugar

1 cup brown sugar, firmly packed

2 eggs, beaten

1 cup unsweetened applesauce

4 cups all-purpose flour

2 tsp cinnamon

1 tsp baking soda

1 tsp salt

1 tsp nutmeg

1 tsp mace

1/2 tsp cloves

1 1/2 cups seedless raisins

1/2 cup mixed candied fruit

1/2 cup candied cherries, sliced

1/2 cup walnuts or pecans, chopped

Preheat oven to 400°F. Cream butter and sugars until light and fluffy. Add eggs and applesauce and beat well. Sift flour, cinnamon, baking soda, salt, nutmeg, mace, and cloves. Add to creamed mixture and blend thoroughly. Stir in raisins, mixed fruit, cherries, and nuts. Drop by teaspoonfuls on an ungreased cookie sheet. Leave about 2 inches between cookies for room to spread. Bake for 15 minutes.

APPLESAUCE-CORNFLAKE COOKIES

3/4 cup shortening

1 cup granulated sugar

1 large egg

1 3/4 cups all-purpose flour

1/2 tsp baking powder

1 tsp baking soda

1/4 tsp salt

1 tsp cinnamon

1/2 tsp cloves

1/2 tsp nutmeg

1 cup sweetened applesauce

1/2 cup seedless raisins

1 cup cornflakes, crushed

Preheat oven to 375°F. Cream shortening and sugar until light and fluffy. Add egg and beat well. Sift flour, baking powder, baking soda, salt, cinnamon, cloves, and nutmeg. Add to creamed mixture alternately with applesauce. Stir in raisins and corn flakes. Drop by teaspoonfuls onto greased cookie sheets. Bake 10 to 12 minutes.

APPLE SQUARES

BASE:

1 cup all-purpose flour

2 tbsp brown sugar

1/3 cup butter, softened

FILLING:

1/2 cup granulated sugar

1 egg

1 tbsp butter

1 cup apples, pared, cored, and finely grated

juice of 1 lemon

pinch of salt

TOPPING:

1 egg, beaten

1 tbsp butter, melted

3/4 cup granulated sugar

1/4 cup coconut

Base: Preheat oven to 325°F. Combine flour, brown sugar, and butter. Mix until crumbly and press in an 8-inch square cake pan. Bake for 10 minutes, then remove from oven and cool slightly.

Filling: While base is cooking, combine filling ingredients in a saucepan. Cook over medium heat until thick, stirring often. Increase oven heat to 350°F. Pour filling over cooked base.

Topping: Combine beaten egg, butter, sugar, and coconut; spread over filling. Bake 20 to 25 minutes.

These squares are delicious as they are, but for a variation, you might like to try them with a lemon icing.

IRISH APPLE SQUARES

This recipe from Hilary Montgomery of Ireland calls for mixed spice, available at most grocery and health food stores.

3 large dessert apples, pared, cored, and coarsely grated

2 tbsp lemon juice

2 tbsp butter

2/3 cup soft brown sugar

3 eggs, beaten

2 1/2 cups whole wheat flour

1/2 tsp baking powder

rind of 1/2 lemon, grated

1/2 tsp mixed spice

1/8 cup raisins

1 tbsp blanched almonds, finely chopped

1/3 cup plus 1 tbsp milk

flaked almonds for decoration, if desired

Preheat oven to 375°F. Grease and line a deep 8-inch square cake tin. Mix apples and lemon juice. Cream butter and sugar until light and fluffy. Add eggs. Stir in flour, baking powder, lemon rind, spice, raisins, and almonds, along with enough milk to make a soft batter. Spread in prepared cake pan, and sprinkle with flaked almonds for decoration if desired. Bake 50 to 60 minutes, until golden and firm. Cut into 9 squares when cold. Serve plain, or split and buttered.

CHEESE-APPLE SQUARES

Probably the oldest recipe in my collection, these squares have been a family favourite for several generations.

1 1/2 cups all-purpose or unbleached flour

2 tbsp granulated sugar

1 tsp baking powder

1/2 cup butter

1 cup cheddar cheese, finely grated

1 cup apple jelly

Preheat oven to 350°F. Combine flour, sugar, baking powder, and butter in mixing bowl. Mix with a pastry blender until crumbly. Add grated cheese. Put half mixture in bottom of an 8-inch square cake pan. Spread with apple jelly. Cover with remaining crumbs. Press lightly. Bake for approximately 30 minutes. Do not overcook.

Note: I like to save time by mixing these squares in a food processor. Just put all dry ingredients in the processor bowl and whirl for a few seconds.

APPLE-DATE SQUARES

Johnny Appleseed would have approved of these tasty bar cookies from BC Tree Fruits Limited.

2 apples, coarsely chopped

2/3 cup water

1/2 cup dates, coarsely chopped

1/2 cup granulated sugar

1 1/2 cups all-purpose flour

1/2 tsp salt

3/4 cup brown sugar, firmly packed

1 1/2 cups quick-cooking rolled oats

1/2 cup walnuts, coarsely chopped

3/4 cup butter, melted

Preheat oven to 350°F. Line a 9-inch square pan with foil or waxed paper; grease lightly. In medium saucepan, combine apples, water, dates, and sugar. Bring to a boil, stirring occasionally. Continue cooking 10 to 12 minutes, until thickened. Cool. In a medium bowl, combine flour, salt, sugar, oats, and nuts. Add melted butter and stir until completely mixed. Reserve 1 cup crumbs. Press remaining crumbs onto bottom of prepared pan, forming a smooth layer. Cover crust with apple mixture. Sprinkle reserved crumbs on top. Bake 45 minutes. Cool in pan. Invert on cookie sheet, remove foil, and invert again. Refrigerate for easy cutting.

APPLE & ORANGE-YOGURT SQUARES

1 cup apples, pared and grated

3/4 cup orange-flavoured yogurt

2 eggs

1/3 cup vegetable oil

1/3 cup milk

2 cups whole wheat flour

1 cup all-purpose flour

1/2 cup granulated sugar

1 tsp baking powder

2 tsp baking soda

1 tsp salt

1/2 cup raisins

1/4 cup nuts, chopped (optional)

Preheat oven to 350°F. Grease 13 x 9-inch cake pan. Combine apples, yogurt, eggs, oil, and milk. Sift flours, sugar, baking powder, baking soda, and salt. Add to apple mixture. Stir until moistened; add raisins and nuts. Mix well. Spread in prepared pan and bake 30 to 35 minutes.

ROLLED OAT–APPLE SQUARES

A great lunch box treat from the New Brunswick Apple Marketing Board.

1 3/4 cups quick-cooking rolled oats

1 1/2 cups all-purpose flour

1/4 tsp baking soda

1 cup brown sugar

3/4 cup butter

3 cups apples, pared, cored, and sliced

1 tbsp butter

2 tbsp granulated sugar

1 tsp cinnamon

Preheat oven to 350°F. Butter 9-inch square pan. Combine oats, baking soda, and brown sugar in a large bowl. Mix in butter. Pat half the oat mixture onto bottom of cake pan. Arrange apple slices over top and dot with 1 tbsp butter. Mix together granulated sugar and cinnamon, and sprinkle over apples. Top with remaining oat mixture. Bake for 40 minutes or until golden brown. Cut into squares to serve.

Variation: May be served hot as a dessert with whipped cream or ice cream.

APPLESAUCE NUGGETS

1/2 cup shortening

1/2 cup granulated sugar

1/2 cup molasses

1 egg, unbeaten

2 cups all-purpose flour

1 tsp baking soda

1 tsp salt

2 tsp cinnamon

1/2 tsp cloves

1/2 cup applesauce

3/4 cup seeded raisins, chopped

1/2 cup peanuts, finely chopped

Preheat oven to 400°F. Cream shortening, sugar, and molasses. Beat in egg. Sift flour, baking soda, salt, cinnamon, and cloves. Add to creamed mixture alternately with applesauce. Stir in raisins and nuts. Drop by rounded teaspoonfuls onto a lightly greased cookie sheet. Bake 10 to 12 minutes.

CHEWY APPLE BARS

Apples, coconut, and raisins give these bar cookies a chewy texture that's sure to be a hit. Great in lunch boxes, and reminiscent of the old favourite, "Chinese Chews."

1 cup whole wheat flour

1/4 tsp baking powder

1/2 tsp salt

1/4 cup vegetable oil

3/4 cup granulated sugar

2 eggs, well beaten

3/4 cup chocolate chips

1/3 cup raisins

2/3 cup dried apples, chopped

1/3 cup coconut

Preheat oven to 350°F. Grease 8-inch square cake pan. Mix flour, baking powder, and salt in a bowl. Add remaining ingredients all at once and stir until mixed. Pour into cake pan and bake 25 to 30 minutes. Cut into bars while still warm. For a variation, roll bars in icing sugar or granulated sugar while still warm.

APPLE PUFF BARS

2 1/2 cups all-purpose flour

2 tbsp granulated sugar

1/2 tsp salt

1 cup shortening

1 egg yolk

2/3 cup milk

1 cup cornflakes cereal, crushed slightly

4 1/2 cups apples, pared, cored, and thinly sliced

1 cup granulated sugar

1 tsp cinnamon

1 egg white

1 cup icing sugar

2–3 tbsp lemon juice

Preheat oven to 375°F. Lightly grease 13 x 9-inch cake pan. Combine flour, 2 tbsp sugar, and salt. Cut in shortening until mixture is crumbly. Add egg yolk and milk, and mix with a fork until mixture holds together. Divide batter into 2 portions. On a lightly floured surface, roll out first portion to cover the bottom of prepared pan; put in pan. Sprinkle with cornflakes. Spread apples over base, and sprinkle with sugar and cinnamon. Roll out remaining batter and place over the filling, pressing it lightly into the pan. Beat egg white with a fork, and brush over top of batter. Bake 35 to 40 minutes. When still warm, drizzle with a mixture of icing sugar and lemon juice.

Note: If apples are very tart, you may need to add a bit more sugar.

LEMON-GLAZED FRUIT & NUT BARS

This delicious recipe was given to me by my sister, Cheryl Hessell.

BARS:

1/2 cup shortening

1 cup granulated sugar

1 egg

1/2 tsp vanilla

1 cup applesauce

2 cups all-purpose flour

1 tsp baking soda

1 tsp cinnamon

1 tsp salt

1/4 tsp nutmeg

1 cup raisins

1 cup walnuts, chopped

GLAZE:

1 cup icing sugar

lemon juice, to give
  spreading consistency

Bars: Preheat oven to 375°F. Lightly grease a jelly roll pan or medium-sized cookie sheet. Cream shortening and sugar until fluffy. Beat in egg and vanilla. Stir in applesauce. Sift flour, baking soda, cinnamon, salt, and nutmeg; add to creamed mixture. Fold in raisins and walnuts. Spread evenly in prepared pan. Bake for 20 minutes.

Glaze: Mix icing sugar and lemon juice together to make lemon glaze. Drizzle bars with glaze while still warm.

APPLE BUTTER TRICORNS

A lovely English recipe that uses self-raising flour. I've included the flour recipe for those who don't have one.

4 eggs

1 cup corn oil margarine, melted

3/4 cup granulated sugar

rind of 1 orange, finely grated

5 cups self-raising flour (see below)

4 rounded tsp Apple Butter (see page 213 for recipe)

Beat eggs slightly. Add margarine a bit at a time, along with sugar and orange rind, beating continuously until mixture is thick. Gently fold in flour. Do not beat. Chill for 1 1/2 to 2 hours, until firm. Divide dough into 4 equal portions. Roll each portion of dough to 1/4-inch thickness. Cut with a large cookie cutter (should be at least 3 inches in diameter). Place circle of dough on a greased cookie sheet. Spoon a rounded teaspoon of apple butter onto centre of cookie. Bring up edges of dough almost to the centre of cookie, forming a 3-sided cookie with some of the apple butter showing in the centre. Pinch each seam to seal. Preheat oven to 350°F and bake for 18 to 20 minutes, until golden brown.

SELF-RAISING FLOUR

4 lbs all-purpose flour

2 tbsp baking soda

4 tbsp cream of tartar

Combine all ingredients and mix thoroughly. This flour will keep in a covered container for several weeks.

MICROWAVE APPLE FUDGE BROWNIES

Who can resist fudgy brownies? This recipe from the Nova Scotia Department of Agriculture and Marketing has got to be the quickest and best ever.

1/2 cup butter or margarine

1/3 cup cocoa

1 cup brown sugar

1/2 cup applesauce

1 tsp vanilla

2 eggs

1 cup all-purpose flour

1 tsp baking powder

1 cup apples, pared, cored, and finely chopped

In a glass bowl, melt butter, add cocoa, and blend. Add sugar, applesauce, eggs, and vanilla; mix. Gradually add flour mixed with baking powder. Add a little milk if batter seems too thick. Add apples, and pour batter into greased 8-inch microwave baking dish. Set power select to medium and microwave for approximately 10 minutes. Let stand to cool for 5 minutes. Cool uncovered. Ice with chocolate or mint icing, if desired.

MARY'S MERINGUES

Apple jelly topped with fluffy meringue makes a delightful square that's both attractive and delicious.

BASE:

1/2 cup butter or margarine

1/2 cup icing sugar

2 eggs

1 cup all-purpose flour

MERINGUE:

2 egg whites

1/2 cup granulated sugar

shake of cinnamon

1 cup walnuts, ground fine

1 scant cup apple jelly

Base: Preheat oven to 350°F. Cream butter and sugar until light and fluffy. Beat in eggs. Add flour and mix well. Press in bottom of ungreased 13 x 9-inch cake pan. Bake 10 minutes. Remove from oven and cool slightly.

Meringue: Beat egg whites until stiff. Gradually add sugar and cinnamon, and beat until glossy. Fold in ground nuts.

Spread apple jelly over base. Cover with meringue. Return to oven and bake until topping is golden brown, about 25 to 30 minutes. Cut into bars while still slightly warm.

CAKES

Throughout history, baking cakes has been a test of one's ability as a cook. Each community had cooks known for their particular "trademark" cake. And there is indeed something very satisfying about making your own cakes.

There's really no mystery to cakemaking—it's easy when you follow a few simple instructions: assemble ingredients and utensils, have ingredients at room temperature, pre-heat the oven, and prepare pans. Measure carefully and follow the recipe.

I am confident that whether you want a special-occasion cake or a quick treat to soothe a child's sweet tooth, you'll find at least one recipe in these pages that fits the bill!

APPLE-CARROT LAYER CAKE

Everyone loves a carrot cake. Grated apples, carrots, raisins, and nuts are some of the ingredients that make this a cake to remember.

CAKE:

1 cup salad oil

1 1/2 cups granulated sugar

3 large eggs

2 tsp vanilla

1 cup apples, pared, cored, and coarsely chopped

2 cups carrots, grated

1 cup golden raisins

1/2 cup chopped pecans (optional)

2 cups all-purpose flour

2 tsp cinnamon

1 tsp baking soda

1 tsp baking powder

1 tsp salt

CREAM CHEESE FROSTING (OPTIONAL):

1/3 cup cream cheese

1/4 cup margarine

1 tsp vanilla

pinch of salt

2 cups icing sugar, approximately

Cake: Preheat oven to 350°F. Grease and flour 2 (8-inch) layer cake pans. Combine salad oil, sugar, eggs, and vanilla in a large mixing bowl. Beat until smooth. Add apples, carrots, raisins, and nuts. Stir to blend. Sift together flour, cinnamon, baking soda, baking powder, and salt. Gradually add to batter in 3 or 4 portions, mixing well after each addition. Spread batter evenly in prepared cake pans. Bake 30 to 40 minutes. Cool in pans a few minutes before removing to a wire rack to cool completely. If desired, ice when cool with cream cheese frosting.

Frosting: Combine all ingredients and mix until smooth. Spread between layers and on top of cake.

FRESH APPLE CAKE WITH CREAM CHEESE FROSTING

Pauline Essery of Summerside, Prince Edward Island, gives us this lovely recipe.

CAKE:

1 1/2 cups all-purpose flour

2 tsp baking soda

1/2 tsp salt

1 tsp cinnamon

1 tsp nutmeg

1/2 cup butter

1 cup granulated sugar

2 eggs

4 cups apples, pared, cored, and chopped

1 cup All-Bran or Bran Buds cereal

FROSTING:

1/3 cup cream cheese

1 tbsp butter, softened

1 tsp vanilla

1 1/2 cups icing sugar

Cake: Preheat oven to 350°F. Grease 9-inch square pan. Sift together flour, baking soda, salt, cinnamon, and nutmeg. Cream butter and sugar until light and fluffy. Add eggs and beat well. Stir in apples, cereal, and flour mixture. Spread in pan. Bake for 45 minutes. Cool to room temperature.

Frosting: Beat cheese, butter, and vanilla. Gradually add icing sugar. Beat until smooth. If frosting is too thick, add 1 or 2 tsp milk. Spread on cooled cake.

PEACHY APPLE CAKE

Peach yogurt is the magic ingredient in this tasty coffee cake.

1 cup all-purpose flour

1 cup whole wheat flour

1/2 tsp salt

1 1/2 tsp baking powder

1 tsp cinnamon

1/2 tsp baking soda

1 cup peach-flavoured yogurt

1/4 cup milk

1/2 cup butter or margarine

1 cup brown sugar

2 large eggs

1 tsp vanilla

3 cups apples, pared, cored, and sliced

2 tbsp butter or margarine, melted

1/2 cup brown sugar

1/2 cup walnuts or pecans

1/4 cup all-purpose flour

1 tsp cinnamon

Preheat oven to 350°F. Grease and flour 9 x 13-inch pan. In a large mixing bowl, combine flours, salt, baking powder, cinnamon, and baking soda. In a smaller bowl, stir milk into yogurt.

Cream butter and sugar until light and fluffy. Add eggs one at a time, beating well after each addition. Stir in vanilla. Stir in grated apple. Spread mixture in cake pan. Combine remaining ingredients and sprinkle over batter. Bake 45 to 50 minutes. Serve warm or cold.

ABC CAKE (ALIAS APPLE BIRTHDAY CAKE)

This cake is baked in 3 layers and put together with creamy butter frosting. It makes a delightful birthday cake or special occasion treat.

APPLE PIE SPICE:

8 tsp cinnamon

2 tsp cardamom

2 tsp allspice

8 tsp nutmeg

CAKE:

1/2 cup shortening

1 3/4 cups granulated sugar

3 large eggs

1 tsp vanilla

2 cups apples, pared, cored, and grated

2 3/4 cups pastry flour

1 tsp baking powder

1 tsp baking soda

1 tsp salt

1 1/2 tsp apple pie spice

1/2 cup milk

Apple Pie Spice: Combine all ingredients. Mix well. Store in a covered spice bottle.

Cake: Preheat oven to 350°F. Grease bottoms of 3 (8-inch) layer cake pans and line with waxed paper. Cream shortening and sugar until light and fluffy. Add eggs one at a time, beating well after each addition. Stir in vanilla and apples. Sift together flour, baking powder, baking soda, salt, and apple pie spice. Add to batter alternately with milk. Beat well after each addition. Divide batter between 3 pans and spread evenly. Bake for 30 to 35 minutes. Cool in pans for 5 minutes before removing to wire racks to cool completely. Remove waxed paper. Put layers together with buttery Cream Cheese Frosting (see page 82).

RAW APPLE CAKE

From the kitchen of Mary Hickey, who serves this delicious cake in her restaurant, Cabot's Reach, in Darnley, Prince Edward Island.

1 cup vegetable oil

2 cups granulated sugar

2 eggs

3 cups all-purpose flour

1 tsp cinnamon

1/2 tsp nutmeg

1 tsp baking soda

1 tsp salt

2 tsp vanilla

3 cups apples, pared, cored, and chopped

1 cup walnuts, chopped

icing sugar

Preheat oven to 325°F. Grease and lightly flour 10-inch angel food pan. Combine oil and sugar. Beat in eggs. Add flour, cinnamon, nutmeg, baking soda, salt, and vanilla. Mix well. Fold in chopped apples and walnuts. Pour into cake pan. Bake for 1 hour. Remove from pan and sprinkle with icing sugar. Makes a lovely dessert, served hot with ice cream.

APPLE-WALNUT BUNDT CAKE

1/2 cup butter

1 cup granulated sugar

1 large egg

1 tsp vanilla

1 2/3 cups all-purpose flour

1 tsp baking soda

1 tsp cinnamon

1/2 tsp allspice

1/2 tsp salt

2 tbsp cocoa

1 cup walnuts, chopped

1 cup applesauce, heated to very warm, but not simmering

Preheat oven to 350°F. Grease and flour 9-inch bundt pan. Cream butter and sugar until fluffy. Add egg and beat well. Stir in vanilla. Sift flour, baking soda, cinnamon, allspice, salt, and cocoa. Sprinkle a bit of this mixture over nuts and toss lightly. Add remaining dry ingredients to creamed mixture alternately with applesauce. Stir in floured nuts. Pour into prepared pan and bake for 40 to 45 minutes.

APPLESAUCE CAKE (WITH VARIATIONS)

1 3/4 cups all-purpose flour

1 tsp baking powder

1 tsp baking soda

1 tsp cinnamon

1/2 tsp salt

1/4 tsp nutmeg

1/2 cup shortening

1 cup brown sugar

1 large egg

1 cup applesauce

Preheat oven to 350°F. Grease and flour 9-inch square cake pan. Sift flour, baking powder, baking soda, cinnamon, salt, and nutmeg. Set aside. Cream shortening and brown sugar. Beat in egg. Add dry ingredients alternately with applesauce. Spread in prepared pan and bake for 35 to 40 minutes.

Variations:
1. Add 1 cup chopped dates to batter.
2. Add 1 cup raisins and 1/2 cup walnuts to batter.
3. Combine 2/3 cup brown sugar, 1/3 cup flour, and 1/4 cup cold butter or margarine. Crumble with a fork and sprinkle over batter before baking.

LEMON-GLAZED APPLESAUCE CAKE

Probably the easiest cake you'll ever make, but don't let that fool you. Your guests will think you made a special effort to create this great cake.

CAKE:

1/2 cup margarine, softened
....
1 cup molasses
....
1 egg
....
1 cup applesauce
....
2 1/4 cups all-purpose flour
....
1 tsp salt
....
1 tsp baking soda
....
1 tsp cinnamon
....
1/4 cup sultana raisins
....

GLAZE:

1 1/2 tsp lemon juice
....
3/4 cup icing sugar
....

Cake: Preheat oven to 350°F. Grease and flour 8-inch square cake pan. Combine margarine, molasses, egg, and applesauce. Beat well with electric mixer. Stir in flour, salt, baking soda, cinnamon, and raisins. Beat briskly for a few minutes. Spread in prepared pan and bake for 45 minutes.

Glaze: Glaze while still warm with a mixture of lemon juice and icing sugar.

APPLESAUCE CHOCOLATE CAKE

This loaf cake needs no icing and is even better after a day or two. Great in lunch boxes or for after-school snacks.

1/2 cup butter

1 cup granulated sugar

1 large egg

1 tsp vanilla

1/2 cup dates, chopped

1/2 cup walnuts, chopped

1 3/4 cups all-purpose flour

1/2 cup cocoa

1 tsp baking soda

1/2 tsp salt

1 tsp cinnamon

1/2 tsp allspice

3/4 cup applesauce

1 square semi-sweet chocolate, coarsely grated

Preheat oven to 350°F. Grease and flour 12 x 4-inch loaf pan. Cream butter and sugar. Beat in egg and vanilla. Stir in dates and nuts. Sift flour, cocoa, baking soda, salt, cinnamon, and allspice. Add to creamed mixture alternately with applesauce. Spread into prepared pan. Sprinkle with grated chocolate. Bake 50 to 60 minutes, until cake tester comes out clean. Remove from pan and cool on a wire rack.

CHOCOLATE CHIP APPLE CAKE

Applesauce and chocolate chips combine with spices, nuts, and raisins for the best lunch box cake ever.

1/2 cup margarine

1 cup granulated sugar

2 eggs

1 1/4 cups all-purpose flour

1 tsp baking powder

1/4 tsp salt

1 tsp cinnamon

1/2 tsp mace

1/4 tsp cloves

1 cup applesauce

1/2 cup raisins

1/2 cup nuts, chopped

1 cup chocolate chips

Preheat oven to 325°F. Grease 9 x 5-inch loaf pan and line with waxed paper. Cream margarine and sugar. Beat in eggs. Sift flour, baking powder, salt, cinnamon, mace, and cloves. Add to creamed mixture alternately with applesauce. Stir in raisins, nuts, and 1/2 cup chocolate chips. Spread into prepared pan. Sprinkle with remaining chocolate chips. Bake for 1 1/4 hours, until cake tester comes out clean. Cool in pan 10 minutes. Remove from pan and peel off waxed paper. Cool completely on wire rack. Wrap in foil and store 12 hours before cutting.

ROSE'S APPLESAUCE CAKE

This applesauce loaf cake comes from the kitchen of Rose Keeping of Dartmouth, Nova Scotia.

1/2 cup shortening, softened

3/4 cup granulated sugar

1 large egg

1 cup seedless raisins, chopped

1 cup walnuts, chopped

2 cups all-purpose flour

1 tsp salt

1 tsp baking soda

1 tsp cinnamon

1/4 tsp cloves

1 cup applesauce

Preheat oven to 350°F. Grease and flour 9 x 5-inch loaf pan. Cream shortening and sugar; add egg and beat until light. Combine raisins, walnuts, flour sifted with salt, baking soda, cinnamon, and cloves. Add to creamed mixture alternately with applesauce, beating well after each addition. Spoon into prepared pan and bake for 1 1/4 hours or until cake tester comes out clean. Cool in pan for 5 minutes before turning out on a wire rack to cool completely.

FUDGY APPLE CAKE

A creamy fudge topping makes this recipe a cake and candy combination that's sure to be welcomed at any time.

CAKE:

1 1/4 cups vegetable oil

2 cups granulated sugar

3 eggs

1 tsp vanilla

3 cups apples, pared, cored, and chopped

3 cups cake and pastry flour

1 tsp salt

1 tsp baking soda

1 cup walnuts, chopped

TOPPING:

1/2 cup butter

1/2 cup evaporated milk

2 cups brown sugar

1/2 tsp vanilla

icing sugar

Cake: Preheat oven to 325°F. Grease and flour a large cake pan, 9 x 13 inches or larger. Beat oil, sugar, eggs, and vanilla with a wire whisk. Stir in apples. Sift flour, salt, and baking soda. Toss in nuts. Add to egg mixture and mix well. Bake for approximately 1 hour, until apples are tender and tests indicate that the cake is done.

Topping: Combine butter, milk, and sugar in a saucepan. Heat over medium heat until mixture comes to a boil. Cook until sugar is dissolved. Remove from heat. Add 1/2 tsp vanilla and enough icing sugar to give consistency for spreading. Spread on cake.

ROMAN APPLE CAKE

An old-fashioned crumb cake at its best.

CAKE:

1 cup granulated sugar

1 1/2 cups all-purpose flour

1/4 tsp salt

1/2 tsp baking powder

1 tsp baking soda

1/2 cup soft shortening

1/2 cup milk

1 egg

2 cups apples, pared, cored, and finely chopped

TOPPING:

1/2 cup brown sugar

2 tbsp margarine

2 tsp all-purpose flour

2 tsp cinnamon

1/2 cup walnuts, chopped

Cake: Preheat oven to 350°F. Grease 9 x 13-inch pan and dust with flour. Sift sugar, flour, salt, baking powder, and baking soda into a large mixing bowl. Add shortening, milk, egg, and apples. Mix on medium speed until well blended. Spread in prepared pan. Sprinkle with topping and bake for 45 minutes.

Topping: Combine sugar, margarine, flour, cinnamon, and nuts. Mix well using a fork or pastry blender.

WILLIE'S DUTCH APPLE CAKE

From the kitchen of one of our Island apple growers, Willie Hekman of Cackleberry Farms, Grand River, Prince Edward Island.

1/4 cup margarine

1 1/2 cups granulated sugar

1 tsp vanilla

2 eggs

2 cups all-purpose flour

2 tsp baking powder

1/2 cup milk

8 apples, pared, cored, and sliced

3 tbsp granulated sugar

1 cup raisins

1 tbsp vanilla

3/4 cup granulated sugar

1/4 cup margarine

3/4 cup all-purpose flour

Preheat oven to 350°F. Grease and flour 9 x 13-inch cake pan. Cream margarine and sugar. Beat in vanilla and eggs. Add flour, baking powder, and milk. Mix well and spread in prepared pan. Combine apples, 3 tbsp sugar, raisins, and vanilla. Spread over bottom layer of batter. Mix together remaining sugar, margarine, and flour, and sprinkle over top of apple mixture. Bake for 1 1/4 to 1 1/2 hours.

I have served this cake hot or cold with whipped cream, ice cream, or plain. Any way you serve it, it's scrumptious.

APPELTAART (DUTCH APPLE CAKE)

A traditional recipe from Holland that's popular the world over.

BATTER:

1/2 cup butter

1/2 cup granulated sugar

3 large eggs

grated rind of 1/2 lemon

1 1/2 cups all-purpose flour

1 1/2 tsp baking powder

FILLING:

5 medium apples, pared, cored, and sliced

1/3 cup brown sugar

1/2 tsp cinnamon

Batter: Preheat oven to 325°F. Grease 8-inch square cake pan. Cream butter and sugar; add eggs one at a time, and beat well after each addition. Add lemon rind. Sift flour and baking powder. Fold gradually into creamed mixture. This makes a thick batter. Spread half batter in cake pan.

Filling: Combine filling ingredients. Toss lightly and spread half mixture over batter. Cover with remaining batter and top with remaining apples. Bake for 1 hour.

GERMAN APPLE CAKE

This recipe comes from my friend Inga-Lill Harding, who has lived and travelled in different countries of Europe and now makes her home in California. As the name states, this recipe comes from Germany.

CAKE:

5 medium apples (use a tart baking variety)

5 tbsp granulated sugar

2 tsp cinnamon

3 cups all-purpose flour

2 1/2 cups granulated sugar

1/2 tsp salt

4 eggs

1 cup vegetable oil

2 tsp vanilla

1/2 cup orange juice

1 1/2 tsp baking soda

1 1/2 tsp baking powder

GLAZE:

1 cup icing sugar

1 tbsp butter or margarine

1/2 tsp vanilla

1–2 tbsp water

Cake: Preheat oven to 350°F. Grease and flour 10-inch bundt or tube pan. Peel apples, core, and thinly slice. Place apple slices in a bowl and toss with sugar and cinnamon. Set aside. In a large bowl, combine flour, sugar, salt, eggs, oil, vanilla, orange juice, baking soda, and baking powder. With an electric mixer, blend together for 1 minute. Scrape down sides of bowl with a rubber spatula; increase mixer speed to medium and blend 3 minutes. You will have a very thick batter.

Put 1/3 batter in pan and cover with 1/2 apple mixture. Drain remaining apples and stir juice into remaining batter. Put 1/2 remaining batter over the apples in the pan, then top batter layer with remaining apples. Again pour any juice into remaining batter, and stir well before spreading over last apple layer. You will end up with 3 layers of batter and 2 layers of apples. Bake for 1 1/2 to 1 3/4 hours until cake tester, when inserted in centre, comes out clean. Cool on rack for 10 minutes. Invert cake and remove pan. Allow to cool completely on wire rack.

Glaze: Mix 1 cup icing sugar, 1 tbsp butter, 1/2 tsp vanilla, and enough water to give icing a smooth consistency. Drizzle over cooled cake.

AEBLEKAGA (DANISH APPLE CAKE)

The Danes are known the world over for their rich, buttery pastries. Apples are used in many of their pastries and desserts. This recipe for Aeblekaga combines apples with a golden butter cake that's sure to become a favourite. Thank you, Inga-Lill Harding, for this lovely recipe.

3/4 cup butter, softened

3/4 cup granulated sugar

3 large eggs

1 tsp vanilla

1 1/2 cups all-purpose flour

1/2 tsp baking powder

5 large apples (Granny Smith or Golden Delicious are preferred)

2 tbsp butter, melted

2 tbsp granulated sugar

Preheat oven to 400°F. Grease 9-inch square cake pan. Cream butter and sugar until well blended. Add eggs one at a time, and beat well after each addition. Beat in vanilla. Sift flour and baking powder. Stir into butter mixture. You will have a stiff batter, which should then be spread into prepared pan. Peel and core apples. Cut apples in half lengthwise and then cut each half into thin horizontal slices, keeping the apple shape. Press sliced apple halves (keeping the slices together) one at a time into cake batter, flat side down. Leave some exposed batter between halves. Sprinkle apples with melted butter and sugar. Bake 30 to 35 minutes, until apples are tender. Serve warm, with ice cream if desired.

APPLE BUTTER CAKE

I came up with this recipe one year when I had an abundance of apple butter. It became my husband's favourite cake when topped with Browned Butter Frosting.

CAKE:

1/2 cup margarine

1 cup granulated sugar

1 egg

1 1/3 cups flour

1 tsp baking soda

1/2 tsp salt

1/2 tsp cinnamon

1/4 tsp cloves

1 cup rolled oats

1/4 cup walnuts, finely
  chopped

1 cup Apple Butter (see
  page 213 for recipe)

BROWNED BUTTER
  FROSTING:

2 1/2 tbsp soft butter

1 1/2 cups icing sugar

3/4 tsp vanilla

1 1/2 tbsp light cream

walnuts, chopped
  (optional)

Cake: Preheat oven to 350°F. Grease and flour 8-inch square cake pan. Cream margarine and sugar until light and fluffy. Beat in egg. Sift flour, baking soda, salt, cinnamon, and cloves. Add rolled oats and nuts, and mix lightly. Stir into creamed mixture alternately with apple butter. Spread in prepared pan and bake approximately 30 to 40 minutes, until cake tester comes out clean. Cool on wire rack.

Frosting: Melt butter over low heat and cook until very lightly browned. Stir in remaining ingredients. Beat until creamy and spread over cooled cake. Sprinkle with chopped walnuts, if desired.

APPLE BUTTER–PECAN CAKE

This cake has a pound cake texture flavoured with apple butter, spices, pecans, and a brandy icing.

CAKE:

1/2 cup butter

1 cup granulated sugar

3 large eggs

2 1/2 cups all-purpose flour

1 1/2 tsp baking soda

1/2 tsp salt

1/2 tsp cinnamon

1/4 tsp nutmeg

1/8 tsp cloves

1 cup buttermilk

1 cup Apple Butter (see page 213 for recipe)

1/4 cup pecans, finely chopped

ICING:

3 tbsp butter, softened

2 cups icing sugar

1/2 tsp brandy extract

2–3 tbsp light cream or milk

Cake: Preheat oven to 350°F. Grease and flour 10-inch square cake pan. Cream butter and sugar until light and fluffy. Add eggs one at a time and beat well after each addition. Sift flour, baking soda, salt, cinnamon, nutmeg, and cloves. Add to creamed mixture alternately with buttermilk and apple butter. Stir in pecans last. Bake 35 to 45 minutes until cake tester comes out clean. Cool completely on a wire rack.

Icing: Cream butter, add icing sugar, extract, and as much milk as needed to give icing a smooth consistency for spreading.

APPLE MINCEMEAT CHEESECAKE

1 cup graham wafer
  crumbs

1/4 cup brown sugar

1/4 cup margarine, melted

1 cup cream cheese,
  softened

2/3 cup granulated sugar

2 tbsp all-purpose flour

juice and rind of 1/2
  lemon

1/2 tsp vanilla

2 large eggs

1 cup Apple-Tomato
  Mincemeat (see page
  201 for recipe)

Preheat oven to 325°F. Combine graham wafer crumbs, brown sugar, and melted margarine. Press into a 9-inch springform pan. Bake in preheated oven for 10 minutes. Let cool on wire rack while mixing remaining ingredients. Turn up oven heat to 450°F.

Cream the cream cheese, granulated sugar, flour, lemon juice, lemon rind, and vanilla until smooth and thoroughly blended. Add eggs one at a time, beating well after each addition. Spread over graham wafer bottom. Spread mincemeat over cream cheese mixture. Cut through top mixtures with a knife, being careful not to cut the crust. This will produce a marble-like pattern. Bake for 10 minutes, reduce heat to 250°F, and bake another 20 minutes. Put on wire rack. Run a sharp knife around edge of pan, but do not remove sides until cake is completely cooled. Chill thoroughly before serving. Makes 8 generous servings.

FARMER'S FRUITCAKE

This special cake comes from the kitchen of my late great-grand-mother Maggie Campbell of Irishtown, Prince Edward Island. It's an economical cake that has stood the test for four or more generations.

4 cups apples, peeled, cored, and cut in small cubes

2 cups molasses

2 eggs, beaten

1/2 cup butter or lard

1/2 cup granulated sugar

1 1/2 tsp baking soda

1/4 tsp cloves

1/2 tsp salt

1/2 tsp cinnamon

1/2 tsp nutmeg

4 cups seeded raisins

3/4 cup mixed peel

1 cup walnuts, chopped

3 cups all-purpose flour

Combine apples and molasses in a medium saucepan. Let simmer 2 hours. (A very slow simmer—do not boil!) Cool to lukewarm. Preheat oven to 325°F. Prepare a 10-inch angel food pan by greasing lightly, lining with brown paper, and again greasing the paper, lightly. Add eggs, butter or lard, sugar, baking soda, cloves, salt, cinnamon, and nutmeg. Mix well. Toss raisins, mixed peel, and walnuts in 1 cup of flour. Add to batter along with remaining flour. Pour batter into pan and bake for 2 to 2 1/2 hours. This is a lovely, moist cake that will keep for weeks.

DARK FRUITCAKE

A moist and delicious wedding or Christmas cake. Bake in one large pan, or in smaller loaves for gift giving. Be aware, though, that you'll have to allow some ingredients to stand overnight—so plan to make this cake over two days.

FRUIT MIXTURE:

2 lbs sultana raisins

2 lbs seeded raisins
(cut in halves, if large)

1 1/2 lbs currants

1/2 lb dates, chopped

1/2 lb mixed peel

1/2 lb candied mixed fruit

1 1/2 lbs candied
cherries, halved

1/4 lb candied
pineapple, sliced

3/4 lb blanched
almonds, slivered

1 cup apple jelly

1 cup applesauce

1/2 cup crushed pine-
apple, drained (reserve
juice)

CAKE BATTER:

1 lb butter

1 lb brown sugar

12 large eggs

2/3 cup molasses

4 cups all-purpose flour (divided)

2 tsp cinnamon

1 tsp nutmeg

1 tsp allspice

1 tsp mace

1/2 tsp cloves

1 tsp salt

1 tsp vanilla

1/2 tsp almond
flavouring

2 tsp baking soda,
dissolved in 2 tbsp hot water

1/2 cup fruit juice
(juice drained from pineapple, and apple
or cherry juice to make 1/2 cup)

Fruit Mixture: Combine fruits and nuts. Let stand overnight at room temperature.

Cake: Prepare cake pans by greasing and lining with heavy brown paper, then greasing and flouring the paper. Preheat oven to 250°F when cake is partially mixed. Cream butter and brown sugar until light and fluffy. Add eggs two at a time and beat very well. Stir in molasses.

Sift 2/3 cup flour over prepared fruit mixture and mix lightly to coat. Combine cinnamon, nutmeg, allspice, mace, cloves, and salt with remaining flour and sift twice. Add to egg mixture alternately with fruit juice, baking soda mixture, and flavourings. Finally, stir in floured fruit. Mix well. Spoon into prepared pans, filling to 1 1/2 inches from top of pan. Bake in preheated oven. Large cakes will take 3 to 4 hours, smaller cakes 2 1/2 to 3 hours. I prefer to start the cake at 250°F for the first hour, then increase heat to 275°F for the remaining time.

This cake freezes well, or will keep for several months in a cool place.

Note: Use your preferred size of pans for this recipe. I personally use an 8-inch square fruitcake pan, or a 10-inch tube pan. Many cooks prefer to use 3 to 4 bread pans.

DESSERTS

Desserts are the crowning glory of any meal, yet they are often the most neglected part of today's cooking, shrugged off as empty, excess calories. In this chapter you'll find desserts both tasty and nutritious.

Why not spoil your family and friends just a little with some of these delicious puddings, cobblers, crumbles, and crisps? Don't forget the Apple Dumplings, once thought to be "strengthening to the stomach." Coleridge said, "A man cannot have a pure mind who refuses apple dumplings."

Hide the calorie chart. Let's have dessert!

CRANBERRY-APPLE CRUMBLE

1/2 lb cranberries

1 cup granulated sugar

3 tbsp cornstarch

3 apples, pared, cored, and sliced

juice and grated rind of 1 orange

1/3 cup butter

3/4 cup brown sugar

3/4 cup oatmeal

3/4 cup whole wheat flour

Preheat oven to 350°F. Cook cranberries and sugar over medium heat until the skins pop. Add cornstarch, apples, orange juice, and rind to cranberry mixture. Pour into 8-inch baking dish. Combine butter, brown sugar, oatmeal, and flour. Mix together with a fork until crumbly. Sprinkle over apple mixture. Bake for 35 minutes. Serve warm with whipped cream.

AFRICAN APPLE CRUMBLE

This recipe comes from the Deciduous Fruit Grower in Bellville, South Africa.

6 apples, preferably Granny Smith, peeled, cored, and thinly sliced

1 tsp grated lemon rind

1/4 cup water

1/2 cup brown sugar

1/2 cup butter or margarine

1 1/2 cups all-purpose flour

1/2 cup granulated sugar

1/4 tsp ginger

1/2 cup raisins (optional)

Combine apples, lemon rind, water, and brown sugar in a saucepan. Cover and cook gently for a few minutes. Preheat oven to 350°F. Place apple mixture in a greased pie pan. Rub butter into flour until crumbly. Add granulated sugar and ginger. Mix well. Sprinkle the crumble mixture over apples and press down lightly. Bake for 30 minutes, until golden brown. Serve with cream or ice cream.

THREE-FRUIT CRUMBLE

Apples combine well with most fruits, and here they team up with blueberries and raspberries. Coriander makes a nice change from the usual apple spices.

BASE:

10 medium apples peeled, cored, and sliced (Cortlands are best)

1 1/2 cups blueberries, fresh or frozen

1 1/2 cups raspberries, fresh or frozen

1/3 cup brown sugar

1 1/2 tsp coriander

1 tsp cinnamon

TOPPING:

3/4 cup all-purpose flour

1/4 cup rolled oats

1/2 cup brown sugar

1/4 cup butter or margarine

1 1/2 tsp coriander

Base: Preheat oven to 350°F. Butter a 1 1/2-quart baking dish. Place apples in the bottom of baking dish and cover with a layer of blueberries and then a layer of raspberries. Combine brown sugar, coriander, and cinnamon, and sprinkle over fruit. Set aside.

Topping: In a separate dish, combine flour, rolled oats, and remaining brown sugar. Cut in butter with a pastry blender until mixture is crumbly. Mix in coriander and sprinkle over fruit mixture. Bake 30 minutes. Serve hot with ice cream.

GRAMMA'S APPLE CRISP

This recipe has been passed down for several generations.

6 large apples, peeled, cored, and sliced

1 1/2 cups breadcrumbs (moist)

3/4 cup granulated sugar

1 1/2 tsp cinnamon

1 1/2 tbsp butter

1/3 cup water

Preheat oven to 375°F. Put half prepared apples in an ungreased 8-inch cake pan. Combine breadcrumbs, sugar, and cinnamon. Sprinkle half of this mixture over apples. Dot with half the butter. Repeat layers. Sprinkle water over the top. Cover and bake for 45 minutes. Serve with pouring cream.

APPLE CRISP

There are as many versions of apple crisp as there are cooks. This recipe is probably the one that would be called the "old standby." No special ingredients, just plain apple crisp.

5–6 apples, peeled, cored, and sliced

2 tsp lemon juice (optional)

3/4 cup brown sugar

1 cup rolled oats

1/2 cup flour

1 tsp cinnamon

1/2 cup butter or margarine

Preheat oven to 375°F. Spread apples in 8-inch baking dish and sprinkle with lemon juice. Mix flour, rolled oats, cinnamon, and butter until crumbly. Sprinkle over apples. Bake 40 to 45 minutes. Serve warm.

ZUCCHINI-APPLE CRISP

A recipe from the PEI Department of Agriculture that you'll want to serve over and over again.

BASE:

4 cups zucchini, pared and coarsely chopped

4 cups apple, pared, cored, and coarsely chopped

3/4 cup granulated sugar

1/3 cup lemon juice

1/4 cup quick-cooking tapioca

1/2 tsp cinnamon

TOPPING:

1 1/2 cups brown sugar

1 cup butter

2 cups rolled oats

1 cup flour

1 tsp lemon peel, grated

1/2 tsp nutmeg

1/2 tsp salt

Base: Preheat oven to 375°F. Combine base ingredients and divide into 3 (1-quart) baking dishes.

Topping: Cream brown sugar and butter. Stir in rolled oats, flour, lemon peel, nutmeg, and salt. When mixture resembles coarse breadcrumbs, divide into 3 parts and sprinkle over base mixture in each baking dish. Bake uncovered 35 to 40 minutes, until base is tender.

Serve warm, or store baked in the freezer for up to 3 months. To serve frozen crisp: thaw and reheat uncovered in a 350°F oven.

Note: Zucchini-Apple Crisp reheats well in the microwave. Defrost about 5 minutes and reheat at medium-high for about 4 to 6 minutes.

PEACHY APPLE CRISP

Apples combine with most fruits and are especially good with peaches. This is comfort food at its best.

BASE:

4 large apples, pared, cored, and sliced

4 large peaches, pared and sliced

1/3 cup brown sugar

1 tbsp lemon juice

TOPPING:

2/3 cup oat bran

2/3 cup rolled oats

1/2 cup brown sugar

2 tsp cinnamon

1/2 cup butter or margarine

Base: Preheat oven to 375°F. Combine apples, peaches, brown sugar, and lemon juice and put in bottom of 8-inch square baking dish.

Topping: In a medium mixing bowl, combine oat bran, rolled oats, brown sugar, and cinnamon. Cut in butter until mixture is crumbly. Sprinkle over fruit mixture and bake 30 to 40 minutes, until fruit is tender.

MAPLE APPLE CRISP

The New Brunswick Department of Natural Resources brings us this lovely maple and apple dessert

6 apples

2/3 cup maple syrup

1/2 cup flour

1/2 cup rolled oats

1/2 cup brown sugar

1/4 tsp salt

1/2 cup butter

Preheat oven to 375°F. Arrange apples in 8-inch square baking dish. Pour maple syrup over apples. Combine rolled oats, brown sugar, and salt. Cut in butter until mixture resembles coarse bread crumbs. Sprinkle topping over apples. Bake until apples are tender and topping is lightly browned, about 35 minutes.

PEANUTTY APPLE CRISP

Our children's favourite.

3 cups apples, pared, cored, and sliced

1/2 cup brown sugar

1/2 cup flour

1/8 tsp ginger

3 tbsp butter

3 tbsp chunky peanut butter

Preheat oven to 400°F. Spread apples in bottom of a casserole dish. Combine sugar, flour, ginger, butter, and peanut butter. Sprinkle over apples. Bake 30 to 40 minutes, until apples are tender and top is crisp.

MICROWAVE APPLE CRISP

A popular dessert that's ready in 15 minutes.

4 cups apples, pared, cored, and sliced

1 tsp lemon juice

2/3 cup rolled oats

1/2 cup all-purpose flour

1/3 cup brown sugar

1/8 tsp nutmeg

1/2 tsp cinnamon

1/2 cup butter

Put apples in an 8-inch square microwave dish. Sprinkle with lemon juice. Combine rolled oats, flour, sugar, nutmeg, cinnamon, and butter, and crumble together. Sprinkle over apples. Cover with waxed paper. Cook on high (maximum power) for 8 to 10 minutes. Serve warm with ice cream or whipped cream.

BAKED APPLES

Baked apples with a difference, these ones cook overnight in a slow cooker. Great for breakfast.

6–8 apples, washed, cored, and peeled down 1/3 of the way from the top

1/2 cup brown sugar

1/2 cup sultana raisins

1/4 cup chopped pecans

1 tsp cinnamon

1/2 tsp nutmeg

2 tbsp butter

1/2 cup hot water

Put apples in a slow cooker. Combine brown sugar, raisins, and pecans. Fill centres of apples with this mixture. Mix spices and sprinkle over apples. Put a dot of butter on top of each apple. Add water around the base of the apples. Cover cooker and set at low heat. Cook for 8 hours.

MARK'S BAKED APPLES

Our son Mark made me promise to include this favourite recipe.

4–6 medium apples, cored and pared 1/4 of the way down

1/3 cup raisins

1/2 cup apple or orange juice

1/4 cup granulated sugar

2 tbsp all-purpose flour

1/2 tsp cinnamon

shake of salt

1 1/2 tbsp butter

1 1/2 tbsp peanut butter

3 tbsp peanuts, chopped fine

Preheat oven to 375°F. Place apples in a baking dish. Pour fruit juice and raisins around them. Combine sugar, flour, cinnamon, salt, butter, peanut butter, and peanuts. Mix until crumbly. Spoon into cavity of apples and over the top, making mounds of filling over apples. Bake for 1 hour, basting often with liquid.

Note: I prefer to core apples from the blossom end, and to slip them under the broiler for 3 to 4 minutes at the end of the cooking time.

BAKED APPLE DUMPLINGS

2 cups all-purpose flour

4 tsp baking powder

3/4 tsp salt

4 tbsp shortening

2/3 cup milk

1/2 cup granulated sugar

sprinkle of cinnamon

6-8 apples, peeled and cored part of the way through, from the blossom end

Sift flour, baking powder, and salt. Cut in shortening until mixture is crumbly. Add milk and mix to a soft dough. Turn out on a floured surface and roll into a thin oblong shape, about 12 x 16 inches. Fill apple centres with a mixture of cinnamon and sugar. Cut pastry in sections to cover apples. Place apple in centre of a pastry square and wrap by bringing the points to the centre. Place on a greased baking dish and make an opening in the top of each pastry case to allow steam to escape. Bake at 400°F for 12 minutes, reduce heat to 375°F and continue baking until apples are tender. Serve with pouring cream and a sprinkle of sugar.

STEWED APPLES

6-7 apples, peeled, cored, and thickly sliced

2 tbsp butter

1/2 cup granulated sugar

1/2 cup water

1/2 cup apple juice

1 slice lemon

Sauté apple slices in butter for 2 minutes. Sprinkle with sugar. Add water, apple juice, and lemon slice. Cover and cook slowly until apples are tender.

FRUIT-FILLED BAKED APPLES

A company dish you'll want to serve on many special occasions.

6 large baking apples

1 large banana, cut in small cubes

1 cup cranberries, chopped

1/2 cup granulated sugar

1/2 tsp cinnamon

1/4 tsp vanilla

1/4 cup walnuts, chopped

1/2 cup cranberry cocktail

Preheat oven to 325°F. Core apples to within 1/2 inch of bottom. Do not cut all the way through. (I prefer to core from the bottom and place apples upside down in baking dish). Peel a strip around the top of each apple. Place apples in a 9-inch square baking dish. Combine banana, cranberries, sugar, cinnamon, and vanilla. Fill centres of apples with this mixture. Sprinkle apples with chopped nuts. Combine cranberry cocktail with any excess filling and pour around apples. Bake for 1 to 1 1/4 hours. Spoon syrup over apples.

HONEY OF A BAKED APPLE

The PEI Department of Agriculture sends us this lovely microwave dessert, which can be prepared ahead and refrigerated until serving time.

4 large apples

1/2 cup water

1/2 cup honey

1 tbsp butter

2 tbsp lemon juice

1/2 tsp vanilla

sweetened whipped cream (optional)

Level apples by slicing a piece horizontally across the bottom. Core apples, and puncture the skin in several places. Place apples in a microwave-proof baking dish. Add water. Cover loosely with heavy-duty plastic wrap. Microwave on high for 9 to 10 minutes, turning dish halfway through cooking period. Cool, covered. In a 4-cup measure, combine honey, butter, lemon juice, and vanilla. Microwave 3 to 5 minutes or until mixture is bubbly. Pour hot syrup over apples. Chill. Serve with sweetened whipped cream, if desired.

CINNAMON-APPLE SURPRISES

Makes an attractive addition to a Thanksgiving buffet.

2 cups "Red Hots" cinnamon candies

1 1/2 cups boiling water

8 small apples

1/3 cup cream cheese

1 1/2 tsp mayonnaise

1/4 cup apple juice

2 tbsp chopped raisins

1 tbsp chopped walnuts

Melt cinnamon candies in boiling water. Peel and core apples. Simmer in cinnamon liquid, basting and turning until apples are cooked but still firm. Cream together cheese, mayonnaise, and apple juice. Add chopped raisins and walnuts. Fill apples with cheese mixture. Place on lettuce leaf to serve.

DUTCH APPLE TART

From Willie's Kitchen at Cackleberry Farms, PEI.

PASTRY:

2 3/4 cups all-purpose flour

pinch of salt

1/2 cup plus 3 tbsp butter, cut in small pieces

2/3 cup plus 1 tbsp granulated sugar

2 egg yolks

FILLING:

1 lb cooking apples, pared, cored, and sliced

1/4 cup plus 2 tbsp granulated sugar

juice of 1 lemon

1/8 tsp cinnamon

1/3 cup raisins

1/2 cup ground almonds

1/2 cup ground hazelnuts

water, enough to moisten

FROSTING:

3 tbsp apricot jam

1/2 cup icing sugar

3 tbsp Kirsch

Pastry: Sift flour and salt into a large bowl. Cut in butter. With a fork, mix in sugar and egg yolks to make a soft dough. Refrigerate for 2 hours. Preheat oven to 400°F. On a floured surface, roll out half dough to fit a 9-inch flan tin. Place dough in tin without stretching. Bake 15 minutes, until golden.

Filling: In a medium bowl, mix apples, sugar, lemon juice, cinnamon, raisins, and nuts. Moisten with water to blend. Spoon into pastry shell. Roll out remaining dough to cover filling. Place over filling and seal edges well. Bake for 30 minutes. Cool in tin overnight.

Frosting: Warm jam, brush over top of cake. Blend powdered sugar and Kirsch. Spread over jam.

AUSTRIAN APPLE TART

PASTRY:

1 cup all-purpose flour

1/2 cup granulated sugar

1/3 cup butter

1 scant tsp grated lemon rind

1 egg yolk

FILLING:

3 cups apples, peeled, cored, and thinly sliced

1/4 cup granulated sugar

1/4 tsp allspice

GLAZE:

3 tbsp granulated sugar

1 tbsp cornstarch

1/2 cup water

1 tsp lemon juice

red food colouring

Pastry: Preheat oven to 375°F. Combine flour, sugar, butter, and lemon rind. Cut with a pastry blender until mixture resembles coarse meal. Mix in egg yolk, just until mixture holds together. Press into bottom and sides of an 8-inch spring-form pan. Bake for 10 minutes. Cool while mixing remaining ingredients.

Filling: Combine apples, sugar, and allspice. Arrange decoratively over pastry. Return to oven and bake 40 to 45 minutes. Cool on wire rack while preparing glaze.

Glaze: Combine sugar, cornstarch, and water; cook, stirring constantly until mixture thickens and comes to a full boil. Stir in lemon juice and food colouring. Spoon over apple filling. Cool at room temperature. Serve with whipped cream.

FRENCH APPLE COBBLER

This recipe came from a television show about thirty years ago and is still popular at our house. We prefer to serve this cobbler hot from the oven with ice cream, but it's equally delicious warm or cold.

BASE:

5 cups apples, pared, cored, and sliced

3/4 cup granulated sugar

2 tbsp all-purpose flour

1/2 tsp cinnamon

1/4 tsp salt

1 tsp vanilla

1/4 cup water

1 tbsp butter

TOPPING:

1/2 cup flour

1/2 cup granulated sugar

1/4 tsp salt

1/2 tsp baking powder

1 egg, slightly beaten

2 tbsp soft butter

Base: Preheat oven to 350°F. Combine all ingredients for base and spread in 8-inch square baking dish.

Topping: In a small bowl mix flour, sugar, salt, and baking powder. Add egg and softened butter. Beat rapidly with a mixing spoon until well blended. Drop by spoonfuls over apples. There will not be quite enough batter to cover all the apples. Bake for approximately 30 minutes, until apples are tender and topping is lightly browned.

QUICK APPLESAUCE CRUNCH

A great dessert for unexpected company. Takes only minutes to prepare.

2 cups applesauce

1/4 cup brown sugar

1/4 cup raisins

1/2 tsp cinnamon

1 cup biscuit mix

1/4 cup granulated sugar

3 tbsp margarine

1/4 cup walnuts, chopped

Preheat oven to 375°F. Combine applesauce, brown sugar, raisins, and cinnamon. Spread in 9-inch square baking dish. Combine biscuit mix, sugar, margarine, and nuts. Blend until mixture resembles coarse crumbs. Sprinkle over applesauce and bake until topping is nicely browned.

APPLE GUMSKUDION

I've no idea how this easy dessert received its name. It's been passed down for at least four generations in my husband's family, so I'll give the credit to his grandmother, Minnie Burns.

CAKE:

6–8 apples, peeled, cored, and sliced

1/4 cup brown sugar

1/4 cup butter, melted

1/2 cup shortening

1 cup granulated sugar

2 eggs

1 tsp vanilla

2 cups all-purpose flour

3 tsp baking powder

1 tsp salt

1 cup milk

BROWN SUGAR SAUCE (OPTIONAL):

1 cup brown sugar

2 tbsp flour

shake of salt

1/2 cup cold water

2 cups boiling water

shake of nutmeg

1 tbsp butter

Cake: Preheat oven to 350°F. Grease 9 x 12-inch cake pan. Combine apples, brown sugar, and melted butter. Spread in prepared cake pan. Cream shortening and sugar, beat in eggs and vanilla. Sift flour, baking powder, and salt and add alternately with milk. Mix well. Pour over apple mixture. Bake for 45 minutes, or until tests indicate that cake is done. Serve warm with pouring cream or brown sugar sauce.

Sauce: Combine sugar, flour, salt, and cold water. Mix well. Put in a small saucepan and gradually add boiling water. Cook over medium heat until thickened. Remove from heat and add nutmeg and butter. Serve over warm pudding.

APPLE KUCHEN

This recipe from Germany is as attractive as it is delicious.

3/4 cup butter or
  margarine

3/4 cup granulated sugar

3 eggs

1 1/2 tsp vanilla

2 1/4 cups all-purpose
  flour

1 tbsp baking powder

1/4 tsp salt

1/2 tsp mace

1/3 cup milk

3 cups apples, pared,
  cored, and sliced

1 tbsp granulated sugar

1 tsp lemon rind, grated

1/3 cup apple jelly

1 tsp granulated sugar

Preheat oven to 400°F. Grease 9 x 12-inch baking dish. Cream butter and sugar until fluffy. Beat in eggs one at a time. Add vanilla. Sift flour, baking powder, salt, and mace. Add dry ingredients alternately with milk. Spread batter in cake pan. Arrange apple slices over top of batter, slightly overlapping them. Sprinkle with granulated sugar and lemon rind. Bake until apples are slightly brown and cake tester inserted in middle of cake comes out clean.

Heat apple jelly and 1 tsp granulated sugar to boiling point. Boil 1 minute. Brush over top of cake. Serve warm, with ice cream if desired.

APPLE BREAD PUDDING

There are fresh apples, apple marmalade, and apple juice in this pudding. A must for real apple lovers.

4 cups bread, cut in
  cubes (use bread that's
  a few days old)

2 cups milk, scalded

1 cup apple juice

2 large eggs, beaten

1/2 cup granulated sugar

1 tsp vanilla

1/2 tsp nutmeg

2 tbsp lemon juice

1 tsp lemon rind, finely
  grated

1 cup apples, pared,
  cored, and chopped

1 cup sultana raisins

1/4 cup apple marmalade

Soak bread cubes in milk and apple juice for 15 minutes. Preheat oven to 350°F. Combine beaten eggs, sugar, vanilla, nutmeg, lemon juice, and lemon rind. Mix well, pour over apples, and sprinkle with raisins. Stir lightly to mix. Spread with marmalade. Pour into a casserole dish and set in a larger dish of water. Bake 45 minutes.

Variation #1: For a different texture, use 3 eggs instead of 2 and separate the whites from the yolks. Put yolks in the pudding and beat the egg whites to stiff peaks; fold in beaten egg whites last. Bake as usual.

Variation #2: Mix as in variation #1, using 3 eggs and reserving egg whites. When pudding is almost cooked, beat egg whites until stiff. Gradually beat in 1/4 cup granulated sugar and 1/8 tsp cream of tartar. Spoon meringue on baked pudding and return to the oven to brown the top.

APPLE HALF-HOUR PUDDING

6 medium apples, pared, cored, and sliced

1 cup all-purpose flour

1/2 cup granulated sugar

1 tsp baking soda

2 tsp cream of tartar

1/4 tsp salt

1/2 cup milk

1/2 tsp vanilla

2 cups boiling water

1/2 cup brown sugar, firmly packed

1 tbsp butter

Preheat oven to 350°F. Grease 8-inch square baking pan. Place sliced apples in bottom of prepared pan. Combine flour, sugar, baking soda, cream of tartar, salt, milk, and vanilla. Spread over apples. Combine boiling water, brown sugar, and butter. Pour carefully over batter. Do not mix. Bake for 30 minutes in preheated oven.

APPLE CREAM PUDDING

6 cups apples, peeled, cored, and sliced

1/2 cup granulated sugar

3/4 tsp cinnamon

1/2 tsp nutmeg

1/4 cup butter

2/3 cup granulated sugar

1 egg

1/2 cup all-purpose flour

1/2 tsp baking powder

1/2 tsp salt

1 cup whipping cream

Preheat oven to 350°F. Combine apples, 1/2 cup sugar, cinnamon, and nutmeg. Toss lightly and put in 8-inch square baking dish. Cream butter and 2/3 cup sugar. Add egg and beat until light and fluffy. Blend in dry ingredients and spread over apples. Bake 30 to 35 minutes. Remove from oven. Pour cream over top. Return to oven and bake another 10 minutes, or until top is golden in colour. Serve warm.

APPLE & CARROT CHRISTMAS PUDDING

A lighter-than-usual Christmas pudding that's sure to become a favourite.

1 large apple, pared, cored, and grated

2 carrots, peeled and grated

1 cup golden raisins

1/2 cup fine dry breadcrumbs

3/4 cup all-purpose flour

1 tsp baking powder

1 tsp cinnamon

1/2 tsp baking soda

1/2 tsp salt

1/2 tsp allspice

1/2 tsp nutmeg

1/2 cup margarine, softened

1/2 cup brown sugar

2 large eggs

Grease a pudding mould and put water to boil for steaming the pudding. Measure grated apple and carrot until you have at least 1 1/2 cups. Add raisins and breadcrumbs to apple mixture. Combine flour, baking powder, cinnamon, baking soda, salt, allspice, and nutmeg. Stir until blended. In a separate bowl, cream margarine and brown sugar. Beat in eggs. Stir into flour mixture. Add apples. Spoon into pudding mould. Cover tightly and steam for 2 1/2 to 3 hours. Let pudding stand on a wire rack for 15 minutes before unmoulding. Serve with your favourite pudding sauce.

Note: This pudding may be frozen and reheated in microwave, or put back in mould and heated over simmering water.

APPLE ANGEL PUDDING

CRUST:

1/3 cup brown sugar,
lightly packed

1 tsp cinnamon

1/4 cup graham wafer
crumbs

1/2 cup almonds, finely
chopped

FILLING:

2 tbsp butter, melted

2 1/2 cups apples, peeled,
cored, and sliced

4 eggs, separated

1/2 cup granulated sugar

1/3 cup sour cream

1 tbsp all-purpose flour

1 tbsp grated orange rind

4 tsp orange juice

1/4 tsp salt

Crust: Grease 8-inch square cake pan. Combine all crust ingredients and sprinkle 2/3 of mixture over bottom of prepared pan. Set aside remaining crumbs.

Filling: Preheat oven to 325°F. Melt butter in a heavy saucepan, add apples, and cook, covered, over low heat until tender. Beat egg yolks slightly, gradually adding sugar. To egg mixture, add sour cream, flour, orange rind, and juice, combining well. Add to apples and cook over low heat, stirring constantly, until mixture thickens slightly. Cool.

Sprinkle salt over egg whites and beat until stiff peaks form. Fold into cooled apple mixture. Pour over crumb crust in pan and sprinkle top with remaining crumbs. Bake for 45 minutes. Serve warm or cold with ice cream.

STEAMED APPLE MARMALADE PUDDING

1 cup apple marmalade

1/2 cup apple juice

1/4 cup suet, finely chopped

3 cups breadcrumbs

1/4 cup all-purpose flour

1 tsp baking soda

2 eggs, beaten

In a small saucepan, combine marmalade and apple juice. Bring to a boil. Stir in suet and let cool to lukewarm. In a large bowl, combine bread crumbs, flour, and baking soda. Blend in cooled apple mixture and beaten eggs. Mix well. Spoon batter into a greased pudding mould. Cover tightly. Set mould on a rack in a large pot. Pour boiling water to halfway up the sides of the mould. Simmer for 3 hours, adding extra water as necessary. Remove mould from steamer. Let sit 10 to 15 minutes before removing from mould. Serve hot with your favourite pudding sauce or whipped cream.

OLD-FASHIONED APPLE PUDDING

2 eggs

1/2 cup granulated sugar

1 tsp vanilla

1/3 cup flour

1 tbsp baking powder

1 tsp cinnamon

1/4 tsp mace

1/8 tsp salt

3 cups apples, peeled, cored, and chopped

1/2 cup golden raisins

Preheat oven to 350°F. Grease 8-inch square cake pan. Beat eggs, sugar, and vanilla until light. Stir in flour, baking powder, cinnamon, mace, and salt. Mix well. Fold in apples and raisins. Spread in prepared pan and bake 45 to 50 minutes. Serve warm with whipped cream or your favourite pudding sauce.

RHUBARB & APPLE PUDDING

You will want to freeze extra rhubarb in season to have a supply for making this tasty cold-weather dessert.

3 cups rhubarb, sliced

2 cups apples, peeled, cored, and sliced

1 1/4 cups granulated sugar

1/2 tsp mace

1 cup all-purpose flour

2 tsp baking powder

1/2 tsp salt

1 cup brown sugar

2 eggs, beaten

1 tsp vanilla

2 tbsp butter or margarine

pouring cream or whipped cream, to serve

Preheat oven to 350°F. Butter 9-inch square baking pan. Combine rhubarb, apples, sugar, and mace. Toss to blend. Put mixture in prepared pan. Sift flour, baking powder, and salt into a bowl. Mix in brown sugar. Stir in beaten eggs and vanilla. Drop this mixture by small spoonfuls over top of fruit mixture. (The batter will not completely cover the fruit.) Dot with butter. Bake for 35 minutes, or until topping is browned and fruit is tender. Serve warm with pouring cream or whipped cream.

QUICK WHIP

Possibly the second-quickest dessert (the quickest being a fresh apple).

2 cups applesauce

2 tsp lemon juice

1 tsp cinnamon

3 egg whites

shake of salt

6 tbsp granulated sugar

Combine applesauce with lemon juice and cinnamon. Set aside.

Beat egg whites with salt until frothy. Gradually add granulated sugar, and continue beating until stiff peaks form. Gently fold into applesauce mixture. Serve immediately. A little nutmeg grated over the top makes a tasty garnish.

TAFFY APPLES

This recipe comes from a friend, Lorene Waugh, who fondly remembers an elderly lady in Hyde Park serving "oodles of taffy apples" on Halloween.

2 cups brown sugar

1 cup granulated sugar

1/2 cup corn syrup

1 1/2 cups boiling water

2 tbsp vinegar

2 large tbsp butter

1 tsp vanilla

Combine brown sugar, granulated sugar, corn syrup, boiling water, and vinegar in a medium-sized saucepan. Boil briskly, until a few drops of mixture become brittle in cold water (about 30 to 35 minutes). Add butter and vanilla. Have apples washed and prepared, with sticks inserted in the stem ends. Dip as quickly as possible into mixture. Let set on a greased pan. This recipe will make 15 to 18 apples.

Note: You must be prepared to move quickly once the taffy is done, because it sets rapidly.

CANDY APPLES

Candy apples don't necessarily have to come from dusty fair grounds. They're easy to prepare, and just as delicious when made at home.

10 medium apples

2 cups granulated sugar

3/4 cup water

1/2 cup corn syrup

red food colouring

wooden skewers

Insert skewers in apples. Combine sugar, water, and corn syrup in top of double boiler. Heat to boiling and then put over direct heat. Do not stir. Cook to 280°F (use a candy thermometer). Immediately put back over boiling water. Add food colouring. Dip apples quickly. Place on a well-greased cookie sheet.

Note: If you haven't got a candy thermometer, the mixture may be tested by putting a few drops of the hot syrup into ice-cold water. If the syrup separates into hard threads, the mixture has been cooked long enough. Overcooking makes the syrup very brittle.

APPLE ICE CREAM

A delicious recipe from the Canadian Department of Agriculture.

1 tsp unflavoured gelatin

1 tbsp cold water

1/2 cup hot milk

2 cups shredded apples, preferably Spartan or McIntosh

1/2 cup fine granulated sugar

pinch of salt

3/4 cup whipping cream

Combine gelatin and water and let sit 5 minutes. Dissolve gelatin mixture in hot milk. Chill. When mixture begins to set, shred apple. Add sugar and salt, and combine with gelatin mixture. Whip cream until stiff. Fold into apple-gelatin mixture. Freeze to a mushy consistency. Stir well, then freeze until firm.

APPLE RIPPLE ICE CREAM

2 1/2 cups apples, pared, cored, and finely chopped

1/3 cup raisins, finely chopped

2/3 cup brown sugar, firmly packed

1/2 tsp cinnamon

1/4 cup water

8 cups (2 litres) ice cream (vanilla or French vanilla)

In a medium-sized saucepan, combine apples, raisins, brown sugar, cinnamon, and water. Heat to boiling over medium heat, stirring constantly. Cover and reduce heat to simmer. Simmer until apples are tender. Cool thoroughly. Soften ice cream just enough to spread. Spread in a 9 x 12-inch freezer container. Drop apple mixture over ice cream and cut through mixture with a knife to make a ripple effect. Freeze for several hours.

SALADS

Apples are best eaten raw, so what better way to serve them than in salads? Tossed, jellied, plain, or garnished— salads are right at home on any menu. Fresh air stimulates the appetite, and salad is a welcome addition to all outdoor picnics and barbecues. With the year-round availability of apples, the salads in this chapter are sure to become family favourites indoors and out.

Note: Never keep salads at warm temperatures for long periods of time. Toss salads, other than jellied varieties, just before serving, or keep well chilled until serving time.

QUICK FRUIT SALAD

A good recipe for unexpected guests.

3 cups prepared fruit cocktail

1 cup seedless grapes

1 3/4 cups (2 cans) mandarin oranges, drained

2 cups miniature marshmallows

1/4 cup maraschino cherries, halved

3 cups apples, diced

3 firm bananas, sliced

sour cream

Combine all fruit in a large bowl. Serve with sour cream.

POTLUCK SALAD

This salad has been a hit at meetings and potluck suppers.

1 head iceberg lettuce, torn

1/2 cup cabbage, finely shredded

1/2 cup apples, finely chopped

1/2 cup pecans, finely chopped

1 cup cooked turkey, cut in cubes

1/2 cup mayonnaise

1 tsp lemon juice

salt, pepper, and onion salt to taste

Toss together lettuce, cabbage, apples, pecans, and turkey. Combine mayonnaise, lemon juice, and seasonings. Add dressing just before serving and mix thoroughly, or serve as is, with dressing on the side.

CHRISTMAS SALAD

1 cup raw cranberries

juice and rind of 1 orange

1/2 cup granulated sugar

1 small pkg raspberry-
flavoured gelatin

1 cup boiling water

3/4 cup cold water

2 apples, diced

Combine cranberries, juice and rind of orange, and sugar. Whirl in blender until well mixed. Let stand 2 hours. Dissolve gelatin in boiling water, add cold water, and let sit until partially set. Fold in cranberry mixture and apples. Spoon into jelly mould; refrigerate until thoroughly set.

Note: This salad can be served with salad dressing or mayonnaise as a main course accompaniment, or with whipped cream as a dessert.

WALDORF SALAD

This Waldorf salad is served frozen, so it must be prepared ahead of time.

2 eggs, slightly beaten

1/4 cup granulated sugar

1/2 cup pineapple juice

1/4 cup lemon juice

1/2 cup celery, chopped

2 cups apples, finely
chopped

1/2 cup walnuts, chopped

1/2 cup crushed pineap-
ple, drained

salt to taste

1 cup whipping cream,
whipped

Combine eggs, sugar, pineapple juice, and lemon juice in top of a double boiler. Cook, stirring constantly until thick. Cool. Add celery, apples, walnuts, pineapple, and salt. Mix well. Fold in whipped cream. Put in individual moulds and freeze. Serve frozen on lettuce.

WALDORF CRANBERRY SALAD

2 cups cranberry juice

1 small pkg lemon-flavoured gelatin

1/4 tsp salt

1 cup apples, chopped

1/2 cup celery, chopped

1/4 cup walnuts, chopped

Heat juice to boiling. Dissolve gelatin in hot juice. Chill until partially set. Add salt, apple, celery, and walnuts. Pour into mould and chill in refrigerator until firmly set.

TURKEY WALDORF SALAD

This recipe comes from the Canadian Department of Agriculture.

3 cups cooked turkey, diced

1 1/2 cups celery, diagonally cut

1 cup red apples, coarsely chopped

1/2 cup walnuts, coarsely chopped

1 tsp salt

1/2 cup salad dressing

Combine turkey, celery, apples, walnuts, and salt. Add salad dressing and toss. Chill 1 hour before serving.

JELLIED CHERRY WALDORF SALAD

1 small pkg cherry-flavoured gelatin

dash of salt

1 cup water, boiling

2 cups ice cubes

1/2 cup apples, finely diced

1/2 cup bananas, diced

1/2 cup celery, finely diced

Dissolve gelatin and salt in boiling water. Stir in ice cubes until mixture is slightly thickened. Remove remaining ice. Stir in apples, bananas, and celery. Pour into an 8-inch pan. Chill thoroughly. Cut in squares to serve.

JELLIED APPLESAUCE SALAD

1 cup water

2 tbsp cinnamon hearts candy

1 pkg cherry-flavoured gelatin

1 cup boiling water

1 cup applesauce

Put first cup of water in a small saucepan. Add cinnamon candy and cook until candies melt. Dissolve gelatin in the boiling water. Mix candy mixture with gelatin mixture. Cool to room temperature. Add applesauce and refrigerate until firm.

APPLE SURPRISE SALAD

1 large pkg lemon-flavoured gelatin

1 small pkg orange-flavoured gelatin

3 cups boiling water

juice of 2 lemons

2 tbsp cider vinegar

2 cups apples, finely chopped

1 1/2 cups cranberry-orange relish

1 1/2 cups crushed pineapple, undrained

1 cup pecans, chopped

Dissolve gelatin in boiling water. Add lemon juice and vinegar. Cool until very slightly thickened. Stir in remaining ingredients. Let sit in refrigerator until thoroughly set.

APPLESAUCE-CHEESE SALAD

APPLESAUCE LAYER:

3/4 cup water

1 small pkg lime-flavoured
  gelatin

1 1/2 cups applesauce

CHEESE LAYER:

1 tsp unflavoured gelatin

1 tbsp cold water

1/4 cup hot water

2 cups cottage cheese

1/2 cup celery, diced

1/4 cup mayonnaise

Applesauce Layer: Combine water and applesauce. Heat to boiling. Stir in lime gelatin until dissolved. Cool. Pour half mixture into oiled jelly mould. Chill until firm. Leave remaining mixture at room temperature.

Cheese Layer: Soften unflavoured gelatin in cold water then dissolve in hot water. Add cottage cheese, celery, and mayonnaise. Pour over green layer and chill until firm. Add remaining applesauce mixture. Chill thoroughly. Unmould on lettuce to serve.

APPLE & CHEESE TOSS

A lovely festive touch for your holiday menus.

1 cup plain yogurt

1/4 cup liquid honey

2 tsp lemon juice

4 cups red apples, diced
  (preferably Cortland)

1 1/4 cups Colby or
  cheddar cheese, diced

1 cup celery, sliced

1/2 cup walnuts, chopped

3 cups iceberg lettuce,
  torn

Combine yogurt, honey, and lemon juice. Chill 2 hours. Just before serving, combine apples, cheese, celery, and nuts. Spoon into lettuce-lined bowl. Pour dressing over apple mixture. Toss lightly to mix.

APPLE & CELERY SALAD

1 cup celery, chopped
....
2 cups apples, diced
....
1/2 cup broken walnuts
....
juice of 1/2 lemon
....
mayonnaise
....

Combine celery, apples, walnuts, and lemon juice. Mix in just enough mayonnaise to hold ingredients together. Chill.

CRANBERRY-APPLE COLESLAW

1 cup cranberries, chopped
....
1/4 cup granulated sugar
....
2 oranges, peeled and finely chopped
....
1 red onion, chopped
....
4 cups cabbage, shredded
....
1 green apple, finely chopped
....
1/4 cup mayonnaise
....

Combine cranberries and sugar. Refrigerate 30 minutes. In a separate bowl, combine oranges, onion, cabbage, apple, and mayonnaise. Chill 30 minutes. Just before serving, combine the two mixtures.

SOUPS
AND SAUCES

There's an old saying that it takes a real cook to make a good pot of soup. Soups are a tradition in all cultures. They can be made from a variety of the least-tender meats, fish, fruits, vegetables, and seasonings, slowly simmered to extract the maximum nutrition and flavour. There are soups for light lunches, appetizers, main meals, and even desserts. Here you'll find soups for every course and every occasion, featuring a variety of foods that combine deliciously with apples.

You'll also find recipes in this section for sauces, from basic applesauces to Spicy Hard Sauce, all of which add apple flavour to a wide variety of meals.

APPLE-VEGETABLE SOUP

An unusual low-calorie soup that's ready in a matter of minutes. Thank you, BC Tree Fruits Limited, for this great recipe.

4 cups beef broth

1 cup apples, grated
(preferably Spartan)

1 cup cabbage, shredded

1 cup carrots, grated

1 tbsp lemon juice

salt and pepper to taste

Combine all ingredients in a soup pot. Simmer 10 to 15 minutes. Vegetables will be tender but crisp. Do not overcook. Serve hot, garnished with apple rings and sprigs of parsley if desired. Serves 6.

APPLE-STILTON SOUP

This recipe from the Ontario Apple Marketing Commission makes a smooth, rich first course. Delicious hot or cold.

1/2 cup butter

2 cups apples, chopped

1/4 cup shallots, chopped

1/4 cup fresh parsley,
chopped

1 tsp fresh basil

pinch of dried sage

3 cups chicken broth

1 cup Stilton cheese,
crumbled

fresh white pepper
to taste

In a heavy saucepan, melt butter; add apples, shallots, parsley, basil, and sage. Cover and cook over low heat until apples are soft. Add chicken broth and simmer gently for 10 minutes. Process in a food processor or blender until smooth. Return to pan. Add cheese and cook over low heat, stirring until cheese is melted. Add pepper to taste.

TOMATO, APPLE & CELERY SOUP

This creamy soup is a Christmas favourite in the home of my friend Hilary Montgomery of Northern Ireland.

1/3 cup butter or margarine

2/3 cup onions, finely chopped

1 1/2 cup tomatoes, pared and quartered

1 1/2 cups celery, cut in 2-inch lengths

1/2 cup dry sherry, optional

1 1/2 cups apples, pared, cored, and quartered

1/2 tsp salt

1/8 tsp pepper

sprinkle of grated nutmeg

1/8 tsp ground ginger

4 cups chicken or turkey stock

apple slices for garnish, if desired

Melt butter in large pan; sauté onions until they begin to brown. Add tomatoes, celery, sherry, apples, and seasonings. Cover and simmer gently for 10 minutes, until buttery. Add stock and simmer gently until tender. Pass soup through a sieve. Put back into pot and reheat to serve. Garnish with apple slices.

APPLE-PARSNIP SOUP

1 1/2 cups leeks, thinly sliced

3 tbsp margarine

1 tsp curry powder

1 1/2 lbs parsnips, peeled and sliced

3 medium apples, peeled, cored, and sliced

4 cups chicken broth (bouillon cubes and hot water can be used)

1 cup milk

salt and pepper to taste

Sauté leeks in margarine over medium heat until softened. Stir in curry and cook for 3 minutes. Add parsnips and apples. Stir in chicken broth and milk. Bring to a boil and reduce heat to a simmer. Cover and cook 40 to 45 minutes, until parsnips and apples are tender. Pour soup into a blender and whirl until smooth. Return to soup pot and reheat. Season as necessary.

Note: For company fare, garnish with Granny Smith apple wedges.

CURRIED APPLE SOUP

A great soup for a cool Halloween evening.

3 tbsp butter

1 medium onion, chopped

1 carrot, chopped

1 stick celery, thinly sliced

1 tsp mild curry powder, or to taste

1 tsp turmeric

1 tbsp all-purpose flour

1 tbsp tomato paste

5 cups chicken stock

2 cloves garlic, crushed

2 bay leaves

1/4 tsp thyme

1/4 tsp oregano

2 large cooking apples, pared, cored, and sliced

salt and pepper to taste

red currant or apple jelly to taste, if sweetener is desired

Melt butter in a large saucepan. Add onions, carrot, and celery. Sauté over low heat for 10 minutes. Stir in curry powder, turmeric, flour, and tomato paste. Cook gently for a few minutes. Gradually add cold stock, stirring constantly until blended. Add garlic, bay leaves, and herbs. Cook about 30 minutes. Add apples to soup and remove bay leaves. Pour soup into a blender and whirl until smooth. Pour into a clean pan and bring slowly to a boil. Add salt and pepper, and sweeten with jelly if desired. Serve hot, garnished with slices of green apple and swirls of sour cream.

Note: For a tart soup, a bit of lemon juice may be added.

CREAMY APPLE & PUMPKIN SOUP

2 tbsp margarine

1 tbsp brown sugar

1 large apple, cored and chopped

1 small onion, finely chopped

2 cups pumpkin, cooked and sieved

2 cups chicken broth

1/2 tsp cinnamon

1/2 tsp salt

1/8 tsp nutmeg

1/8 tsp pepper

1 cup light cream or half and half

In a large saucepan, over medium heat, dissolve brown sugar in margarine. Add apple and onion. Cook gently until onion is soft. Stir in pumpkin, chicken broth, cinnamon, salt, nutmeg, and pepper. Bring to a boil. Boil gently until apples are tender. Remove from heat, and cool to room temperature. Pour about 1 cup at a time into blender container and whirl until smooth. Return to saucepan. Stir in cream, and warm over low heat to serve.

CRANBERRY-APPLE SOUP

The delightful tastes of cranberry and apple combine in this dessert soup that is delicious served warm or cold. My family likes a chilled soup served with whipped cream.

2 cups cranberry sauce, puréed

3 cups apple juice

1/3 cup brown sugar

3 apples, pared, cored, and thinly sliced

1 cinnamon stick (3-inch length)

1 1/2 tbsp cornstarch

1/3 cup water

1 tsp vanilla

Combine cranberry sauce, apple juice, and sugar in a saucepan. Stir over medium heat until sugar dissolves. Add apple slices and cinnamon stick. Bring to a boil; reduce heat and simmer, covered, 8 to 10 minutes. Remove cinnamon stick. Combine cornstarch and water, and stir into hot apple mixture. Return to a boil and cook 1 minute, until mixture is clear and slightly thickened. Remove from heat. Stir in vanilla.

SWEDISH FRUIT SOUP

This recipe from Sweden, properly named Fruktsoppa, combines a variety of dried fruits in a very tasty dessert soup.

1 cup dried apples

1 cup dried apricots

1/2 cup dried peaches

1/2 cup dried pitted prunes

1/2 cup dark seedless raisins

8 cups water

3 tbsp granulated sugar

3 tbsp quick-cooking tapioca

1 tsp grated orange or lemon peel

1 stick of cinnamon

1 cup raspberry fruit syrup

Combine apples, apricots, peaches, prunes, and raisins in a dutch oven or large saucepan. Cover with water and let sit at least 3 hours. Stir in sugar, tapioca, and grated orange or lemon peel. Add cinnamon stick. Let stand a few minutes. Place over medium heat and bring to a boil. Cover and simmer until fruit is tender, approximately 1 hour. Remove cinnamon stick. Stir in raspberry syrup. Cool. Refrigerate and chill thoroughly. Serve with whipped cream, and garnish with blanched almond slivers if desired.

PIONEER CHUCKWAGON STEW

This easy North American recipe is as popular in the kitchens of today as it was on the cattle roundups of yesterday. Great when served with hot, fluffy biscuits.

1 1/2 lbs beef, round steak, cut in strips

2-3 tbsp all-purpose flour

1 tbsp salad oil or shortening

4 cups boiling water

1 bay leaf

3-4 medium onions, peeled and quartered

4 potatoes, cut in 1-inch cubes

2 cups apples, pared, cored, and sliced

2 cups carrots, pared and sliced

1/8 cup butter

Toss beef strips in flour. Brown in salad oil or shortening over medium heat. Add boiling water, bay leaf, salt, and pepper. Cover and simmer 2 hours. Add remaining ingredients and simmer a further 1 1/2 to 2 hours.

BEEF STEW WITH APPLE CIDER

Adding apple cider to stew brings out the flavour in the vegetables.

2 lbs stewing beef, cut in 1-inch cubes

1/4 cup all-purpose flour

salt and pepper to taste

1/4 cup vegetable oil

2 medium onions, peeled and sliced

2 cups sweet apple cider

1/2 cup water

2 tbsp cider vinegar

1/2 tsp dried thyme

2–3 medium potatoes, cubed

4 carrots, peeled and sliced

1 stalk celery, sliced

Toss beef cubes in a mixture of flour, salt, and pepper to coat evenly. Heat vegetable oil in a heavy pot over medium heat. Brown beef cubes, 1/2 at a time. Remove meat from pan and add onions. Sauté until soft. Drain off excess fat. Combine meat with onions. Add apple cider, water, vinegar, and thyme. Bring to a boil; reduce heat and simmer, covered, until meat is almost tender, about 1 to 1 1/2 hours. Add vegetables to stew and simmer, covered, 30 to 35 minutes, until meat and vegetables are tender. Serves 6.

APPLESAUCE #1

Peel, core, and slice desired number of apples. Put in heavy saucepan with small amount of water. Cook over medium-low heat, stirring occasionally to prevent sticking, until cooked through. Mash with potato masher or sieve, if desired. Sugar may be added to applesauce at any time during cooking, or you may prefer to leave it unsweetened.

APPLESAUCE #2

I usually make large quantities of applesauce, and this is my favourite way of making it.

Wash apples, and remove stem and blossom ends. Cut in quarters, or smaller, depending on size of apples. Cook in a heavy saucepan over medium-low heat, with a small amount of water to prevent scorching. When apples are tender, put through a sieve or food mill. This will take out all seeds and peelings. Add sugar to hot applesauce if desired.

Variation: Some people like a small amount of vanilla added to hot applesauce, for a different flavour.

This sauce will have much the same texture as applesauce purchased in a store. It freezes very well for several months. Simply cool sauce and put in freezer containers.

CRANBERRY APPLESAUCE

2 cups cranberries

2 cups apples, peeled and sliced

3/4 cup water

1 cup granulated sugar

Combine all ingredients and cook slowly until tender, about 20 minutes. Cool slightly and beat with an egg beater until fluffy.

OLD-FASHIONED APPLESAUCE

8 medium apples

3/4 cup water

3 tbsp sugar

1/2 tsp cinnamon

Peel, core, and chop apples. Add water, and simmer until apples are tender, about 45 minutes. Add sugar and cinnamon. Stir until dissolved. Serve hot or cold.

Note: I prefer August apples, such as Yellow Transparent, for this recipe; however, most any apple or combination of apples makes good sauces.

APPLE CIDER SAUCE

This sauce is nice served with baked ham.

1/4 cup brown sugar

1 1/2 tbsp cornstarch

1/4 tsp salt

1/8 tsp cloves

1/4 tsp cinnamon

shake of nutmeg

1 1/2 cups apple cider

1 tsp lemon juice

Combine all ingredients, except lemon juice, in a heavy saucepan. Cook over high heat, stirring constantly until thickened and clear. Stir in lemon juice.

NO-COOK APPLESAUCE

Roast pork for supper and no applesauce? Don't worry. Here's a quick solution that takes minutes to prepare.

1 lb apples, peeled, cored, and sliced

1/3 cup corn syrup

2 tbsp lemon juice

1 tbsp granulated sugar

Put about half the apples in a blender, along with remaining ingredients. Cover and blend on high speed until smooth. Add remaining apples, a few at a time, and continue blending. Great served with roast pork.

APPLE BUTTERSCOTCH SAUCE

This sauce should be used immediately, as it will thin if held for any length of time.

1/4 cup butter or
  margarine

1 cup brown sugar,
  lightly packed

1/4 tsp cornstarch

pinch of salt

2 cups apple juice

Melt butter, and blend in brown sugar, cornstarch, and salt. Cook over medium to low heat until slightly browned. Stir in apple juice and continue cooking until thickened. Cook 3 minutes more. Serve on steamed puddings or gingerbread.

Variation: A little water may be used in place of some of the apple juice, for a milder flavour.

APPLE-RAISIN SAUCE

1/4 cup brown sugar

1 cup apple juice

1 tbsp cornstarch

1/4 tsp salt

1/2 tsp cinnamon

1/8 tsp nutmeg

1/2 cup seedless raisins

1 tbsp lemon juice

1 1/2 tbsp butter

Combine sugar, apple juice, cornstarch, salt, cinnamon, and nutmeg. Cook over medium heat, stirring constantly, until mixture is boiling. Simmer about 5 minutes. Stir in raisins, lemon juice, and butter. Cook 2 minutes longer.

SPICY HARD SAUCE

An especially good sauce on apple puddings, although it doesn't contain any apple or apple product in itself.

1 1/2 cups icing sugar

1/4 tsp cinnamon

1/8 tsp cloves

1/8 tsp nutmeg

1/2 cup butter

Sift icing sugar and spices. Cream butter, and add sugar mixture. Blend very well. Chill. Serve on baked or steamed pudding.

MAIN DISHES

The casserole, the "meal-in-a-dish," is the most convenient of all main dishes. Cassroles offer the adventurous cook the opportunity to experiment with various combinations of foods. Here you will find a selection of one-dish meals that are economical, easy to prepare, and will save you time with washing up.

Most casseroles can be frozen, or will keep two or three days in your refrigerator. They are best when cooked until slightly underdone one day, then thoroughly reheated for serving a day or two later. This gives the flavours a chance to blend.

Accompany these tasty dishes with crisp salads, chutney, or crusty breads. This is comfort food at its best, perfect for family fare or casual parties.

APPLE-STUFFED CHICKEN BREASTS

This recipe from the Nova Scotia Department of Agriculture is quick and easy enough for everyday meals, yet elegant enough for entertaining.

4 chicken breasts,
 skinned and boned

1 cup apples, peeled,
 cored, and chopped

1/2 cup mozzarella
 cheese, shredded

1/2 cup dry breadcrumbs

2 tbsp butter or
 margarine

1/4 cup water

1 1/2 cups apple juice

4 tbsp cornstarch

Flatten chicken breasts between sheets of waxed paper. Combine apple, cheese, and bread crumbs; divide between chicken breasts. Roll up each chicken breast; secure with toothpicks. Melt butter in skillet. Brown chicken breasts on all sides. Add apple juice, cover, and simmer 15 to 20 minutes, or until chicken is no longer pink. Remove chicken from pan. Combine 1/4 cup water and cornstarch; stir into juices in pan. Cook and stir until thickened. Pour thickened sauce over breasts and serve.

PORK & APPLE CASSEROLE

6 pork chops, cut thick

3 tbsp vegetable oil

2 medium onions,
 chopped

1 cup long-grain rice

1 1/4 cups apple juice

1 cup water

1 tbsp brown sugar

1 tsp prepared mustard

1 tsp salt

1/8 tsp cinnamon

1/2 cup apples, peeled, cored, and
 chopped

1/2 cup raisins

Preheat oven to 350°F. Brown chops in oil, and set aside. Add onions to remaining fat and cook for 5 minutes, stirring well. Stir in the rice and cook for 3 minutes. Stir in remaining ingredients and bring to a boil. Turn into a greased casserole dish. Top with browned pork chops. Cover and bake for 1 1/4 hours, until chops and rice are tender.

CURRIED STEAK

2 lbs chuck steak, trimmed, and cut into 1-inch pieces

1 medium carrot, chopped

4 sticks celery, diced

1 large onion, chopped

1 apple, peeled and chopped

2 tbsp all-purpose flour

1 tsp salt

2 tsp curry powder

1 tbsp corn syrup

2 tsp lemon juice

1 1/4 cups canned tomato soup

1 cup water

Place steak in a large saucepan. Add carrots, celery, onion, and apple. Mix together flour, salt, and curry powder. Stir in corn syrup and lemon juice. Add to meat and vegetables with tomato soup and water. Mix well. Cover and simmer gently for 2 hours or until meat is tender. Serve with hot rice.

BAKED APPLE CHICKEN

1 chicken (about 3 lbs),
  cut for frying

1/4 cup all-purpose flour

salt and pepper to taste

3 tbsp butter

1/2 cup onion, chopped

1/2 cup green pepper,
  chopped

1 clove garlic, crushed

2 cups apples, peeled,
  cored, and finely
  chopped

1/2 tsp thyme

2 tsp curry powder

2 cups chopped
  tomatoes

3 tbsp raisins

1/2 cup apple juice

Toss chicken pieces in flour, salt, and pepper. Brown in skillet with butter. Put chicken in a 9 x 12-inch baking pan. Drain off excess fat from skillet. Sauté onion, pepper, garlic, and apples. Cook until vegetables begin to soften. Preheat oven to 350°F. Add thyme, curry powder, tomatoes, raisins, and apple juice. Pour over chicken. Bake for 45 minutes, or until chicken is tender.

APPLE MEATLOAF

A meatloaf that's a bit different, made with lean ground pork.

2 lbs lean ground pork

2 slices bread (preferably whole wheat)

1/2 cup milk

1 egg, beaten

1 medium apple, peeled and finely chopped

1/2 cup celery, finely chopped

1/4 cup wheat germ

1 tbsp chopped fresh parsley

salt and pepper to taste

1/8 tsp thyme

shake of nutmeg

Preheat oven to 350°F. Combine all ingredients in a large mixing bowl. Mix well. Spread mixture in a large loaf pan. Bake for 1 hour and 20 minutes.

Variation: For an interesting change of pace, spread a mixture of 1/4 cup ketchup, 2 tbsp brown sugar, and a pinch of nutmeg over top of meatloaf before baking. This makes a nice glaze that turns "plain old meatloaf" into "company cookin'."

APPLESAUCE MEATBALLS

1 lb lean or medium
  ground beef

1 1/2 cups soft
  breadcrumbs

1 egg, beaten

1 cup applesauce

1/4 cup onion, chopped

2 tsp salt

1 cup ketchup

1/2 cup water

1 tbsp lemon juice

1 tsp sweet basil

Preheat oven to 350°F. Combine beef, breadcrumbs, eggs, applesauce, onion, and salt. Shape into walnut-sized balls. Brown on both sides in a skillet. Put in a baking dish. Combine ketchup, water, lemon juice, and basil. Pour over meatballs. Bake uncovered for 1 1/2 hours. Serve with hot rice or buttered noodles.

APPLESAUCE PORK CHOPS

6 pork chops

1 cup applesauce

1/4 cup honey

1 tsp lemon juice

1/4 tsp nutmeg

1/4 tsp cinnamon

Place pork chops in a 9 x 12-inch baking dish. Bake for 30 to 40 minutes at 350°F. Remove from oven, and drain. Reduce oven temperature to 300°F. Put chops back in baking dish. Combine applesauce, honey, lemon, nutmeg, and cinnamon. Pour over chops. Return to oven and bake 15 to 20 minutes.

APPLE-SCALLOP BAKE

1 tbsp butter

1/2 cup onion, finely
chopped

1 lb scallops

2 cups apples, peeled,
cored, and chopped

2/3 cup mushrooms,
finely chopped

1 tsp lemon juice

1 tsp parsley

1/2 tsp salt

1/2 tsp basil

2 tbsp butter

2 tbsp all-purpose flour

1 cup milk

1/4 cup fine dry bread-
crumbs

1 tbsp butter, melted

Melt 1 tbsp butter in skillet. Sauté onion until tender. Add scallops, apples, mushrooms, lemon juice, parsley, salt, and basil. Cook, stirring over medium heat for 6 to 8 minutes. In a separate saucepan, melt 2 tbsp butter, add flour, and stir in milk. Cook until thickened. Pour sauce over scallop mixture. Mix well. Spread in a shallow, greased baking dish. Sprinkle with breadcrumbs and remaining butter. Cook under broiler until browned, 4 to 5 minutes.

APPLE-TUNA CASSEROLE

2 tbsp butter

2 cups apples, diced
(unpeeled)

1 cup onions, chopped

1 cup celery, chopped

1 cup cheddar cheese,
shredded

1 cup milk

1 tbsp cornstarch

1 cup rice

1 3/4 cups canned tuna,
drained and flaked

salt and pepper to taste

3/4 cup breadcrumbs

2 tbsp butter, melted

Melt butter in a skillet. Sauté apples, onion, and celery until tender. With a slotted spoon, remove mixture from pan, reserving fat. Combine shredded cheese, milk, and cornstarch. Cook in skillet, stirring constantly until thickened. Meanwhile, preheat oven to 375°F. Grease a large casserole dish. Combine apple mixture, sauce, tuna, and salt and pepper. Mix thoroughly. Spoon into prepared dish. Mix breadcrumbs with melted butter and sprinkle over casserole. Bake for 25 to 30 minutes, until heated through and browned on top.

SWISS CHEESE
& CHICKEN BAKE

1 broiler chicken, cut in serving-size pieces

salt and pepper to taste

2 tbsp butter

1/2 cup onion, thinly sliced

1 clove garlic, crushed

1/2 cup apple juice

1 tsp parsley

1/2 tsp salt

1/4 tsp thyme

2 cups firm apples, peeled, cored, and cut in wedges

1/2 cup whipping cream

1 cup (4 ounces) Swiss cheese, shredded

Sprinkle chicken pieces with salt and pepper. Sauté in butter until browned on both sides. Remove chicken from pan, and sauté onion and garlic. Put chicken back in pan, and add apple juice, parsley, salt, and thyme. Cover and simmer 15 to 20 minutes. Add apples and simmer until chicken is tender. Arrange chicken and apples in a shallow baking dish. Put cream in skillet and stir to blend in meat and vegetable particles. Pour cream over chicken and sprinkle with Swiss cheese. Place under a broiler until cheese melts. Serve immediately.

APPLE & BACON CASSEROLE

The Canadian Egg Marketing Agency brings us this easy casserole. Cooked pork or cubed ham may be used instead of bacon.

4 cups flat wide egg
  noodles, cooked

4 medium cooking
  apples, peeled, cored,
  and thinly sliced

1/2 lb bacon, fried and
  crumbled

4 eggs

2 cups creamed
  cottage cheese

1/2 cup cream cheese

2 tbsp brown sugar
  or honey

2 tsp cinnamon

1 cup breadcrumbs

2 tbsp butter

Preheat oven to 375°F. Combine noodles, apples, and bacon in a well-buttered 2-quart casserole dish. In a blender or food processor, combine eggs, cottage cheese, cream cheese, sugar, and cinnamon. Pour over apple mixture and top with breadcrumbs and butter. Bake for 30 to 35 minutes.

EASY FRANKS & KRAUT

6 slices bacon, diced

1/4 cup onion, sliced

1 lb (1 can) sauerkraut,
  drained

1 cup apple juice

1 tbsp brown sugar

1 tsp caraway seeds

1 small apple, grated
  (unpeeled)

6 frankfurters

Cook bacon until fat begins to melt. Add onion and cook 3 minutes. Add sauerkraut and cook 5 minutes. Stir in apple juice, sugar, caraway, and grated apple. Simmer, covered, for 30 minutes. Place franks on top of mixture. Cover and simmer until franks are heated through.

SWEET & SOUR SAUSAGE

1 lb hot ground sausage

2 lbs regular ground
   sausage

1 cup cracker crumbs

3 eggs, slightly beaten

1/2 cup apple jelly, melted

6 tbsp apple cider or
   apple juice

4 tbsp soy sauce

1 1/2 cups ketchup

Mix sausage, cracker crumbs, and eggs. Roll into 1-inch balls and brown in skillet. Drain on paper towels. Combine jelly, cider, soy sauce, and ketchup. Return sausage balls to skillet and pour sauce over them. Simmer until heated through. Serve immediately.

PORK ROAST WITH APPLE GLAZE

Nothing goes together better than apples and pork.

1 (5-lb) pork shoulder
   roast

1 tsp pumpkin pie spice

1 cup apple cider

2 apples, cored and sliced

2 tbsp brown sugar

2 tbsp all-purpose flour

2 tbsp water

Preheat oven to 325°F. Brown pork in large skillet. Remove from skillet to roasting pan. Sprinkle on both sides with pumpkin pie spice. Pour cider over meat. Cover and cook for 3 hours, until very tender. Remove meat from roaster and keep warm. Put sliced apples in roaster. Combine brown sugar, flour, and water. Add to roaster, and stir over medium heat until thickened. Pour apple glaze over roast. Serve.

SAUSAGE
& SAUERKRAUT SKILLET

This tasty main dish is cooked entirely in a skillet.
And it's quick to make—ready in just 30 minutes.

1 lb sausage, cut in small
diagonal pieces
....
1 onion, thinly sliced
....
2 cups sauerkraut,
drained
....
1/2 cup apple juice
....
1 1/2 tbsp brown sugar
....
1/4 tsp caraway seed
....
salt and pepper to taste
....
2 apples, cored and sliced
....

Sauté sausage and onion until onion
looks clear. Add sauerkraut and heat
thoroughly. Stir in apple juice, sugar,
caraway, salt, and pepper. Bring to a boil.
Cover and simmer 15 minutes. Add apple
and simmer 3 to 4 minutes, until barely
tender. Serve immediately.

APPLE-STUFFED SPARERIBS

3 lbs pork spareribs, cut
  in serving-size pieces

1/4 cup water

1 cup celery, chopped

1 medium onion, chopped

1 tbsp butter

1 apple, cored and
  thinly sliced

2 cups bread cubes

1/4 tsp rosemary

salt and pepper to taste

1/4 cup chili sauce

Preheat oven to 350°F. Place ribs on rack in 9 x 12-inch baking dish. Add water. Cover and bake for 1 1/2 hours. Cook celery and onion in butter until clear. Add apple and cook 3 minutes longer. Stir in bread cubes, sage, and rosemary. Remove ribs from pan and season with salt and pepper. Combine 1/2 cup drippings with bread mixture to make dressing. Reserve remaining drippings. Shape dressing into patties. Place on baking rack. Combine chili sauce and remaining drippings. Brush ribs on both sides with chili sauce mixture. Place over dressing patties. Bake uncovered for approximately 1/2 hour, brush with sauce, and bake another 20 minutes.

ACCOMPANIMENTS

Whether the occasion is a family breakfast or a party buffet, you can entertain and nourish folks by providing that "little extra." Accompany roast turkey with Apple-Raisin Dressing and serve Sweet Potato Casserole with baked ham; or observe tradition and serve Apple & Tomato Scallop with baked beans. In the pages that follow you'll find a variety of accompaniments, both new and old, to complement any dish.

APPLE-RAISIN DRESSING

This dressing is nice with any poultry. It can be baked inside the bird or in a casserole dish. When baking this dressing in a casserole dish, I like to substitute some of the butter or margarine with the juice from the poultry.

1 1/2 cups celery, chopped

1 medium onion, chopped

1 cup butter or margarine

8 cups soft breadcrumbs

3 medium-sized tart apples, pared, cored, and chopped

1/2 cup seedless raisins

1 1/2 tsp sage

salt and pepper to taste

Preheat oven to 325°F. Sauté celery and onion in butter until tender. Pour into a large mixing bowl. Add remaining ingredients and mix lightly until thoroughly blended. Place in a well-buttered casserole dish. Cover and bake for 20 minutes. Uncover and bake until slightly crisp on top and lightly browned, about another 15 minutes.

SAUSAGE-APPLE STUFFING

This recipe makes enough dressing for a 10- to 12-pound turkey. A nice change from the traditional recipes.

1 lb sausage meat

1 large onion, diced

2 large apples, pared, cored, and chopped

1/2 cup water

salt and pepper to taste

8 cups soft bread cubes

Brown sausage meat in a skillet. If pieces are large, break up with a spoon. Drain well, reserving some of the dripping. Return reserved dripping to pan and sauté onion until clear. Add apple and water. Heat to boiling. Pour over sausage. Add bread cubes. Toss lightly. Sprinkle with salt and pepper. Use to stuff cavity of turkey. Cook turkey in usual manner.

APPLE & CARROT BAKE

Here's a healthy recipe that's easy to prepare. Slip this tasty combo alongside the roasting chicken during the last hour of cooking time.

4 cups grated carrots

1 1/2 cups apples, unpeeled, grated

1/4 to 1/3 cup brown sugar, depending on sweetness of apples

1/2 tsp salt

1/2 cup apple juice

2 tbsp butter

Preheat oven to 350°F. Combine all ingredients in a small buttered casserole dish. Cover and bake for 40 minutes. Stir twice during cooking time. Serve hot.

MIXED-FRUIT STUFFING

I like to serve this tasty side dish with roast pork.

1/2 cup dried prunes, chopped

1/2 cup dried apricots, chopped

2 cups cold water

1 1/2 cups soft bread-crumbs

1 cup apples, pared, cored, and sliced

1/2 cup pears, pared, cored, and sliced

1/2 cup seedless raisins

1/2 cup walnuts, chopped

1/2 tsp salt

1/2 tsp nutmeg

1/2 tsp allspice

1 tsp lemon juice

2-3 tbsp brown sugar

In a medium saucepan, over high heat, combine prunes, apricots, and water. Heat to boiling. Reduce heat and simmer until fruit is tender, about 10 to 15 minutes. Drain well. Place fruit in a bowl. Add remaining ingredients. Mix well. Let sit a few minutes to combine flavours and mix once more before serving. No further cooking is required.

DEUTCH MESS

This very old recipe comes from the Lunenburg County Federation of Agriculture. What could be more Maritime than a combination of potatoes, fish, and apples?

6 medium potatoes, pared and cut in bite-size pieces

1 lb salted codfish, soaked and cut in pieces

1/2 lb salt pork, cubed

1 large onion, sliced

6 medium apples, pared, cored, and quartered

2-3 tbsp granulated sugar

1/4 cup cream

parsley, green pepper, or cooked carrot for garnish (optional)

Boil potatoes until tender. Drain. Place fish in a separate pot. Cover with cold water. Boil until tender. Drain. In a large frying pan, fry pork cubes slowly until golden brown. Leave in frying pan. Add onion, and sauté until clear. Stir in apples. Sprinkle with sugar. Cover and let cook until apples are tender.

Spread potatoes in a serving dish, cover with fish, and slide the mixture from the frying pan over the top. Dribble with cream, and garnish with parsley, green pepper, or cooked carrot if desired.

Variations:
1. Leave out fish, and this dish is called "Potatoes and Apples."
2. Replace fish with 2 cups cooked carrot strips for "Geese Feed."
3. Leave out the apples and you have "House Bankin'."

MOM'S RED CABBAGE & APPLE

I can't imagine red cabbage without apple. I have various recipes using this combination, but for me, Mom's (Helen Murphy of Delta, BC) is the easiest and best.

4 cups shredded
  red cabbage

1/2 cup boiling water

1 tsp salt

1 large apple, grated

1/4 cup brown sugar

1/4 cup cider vinegar

3 whole cloves

1 tbsp butter

Boil cabbage in salted water for 10 minutes. Do not overcook. Stir in remaining ingredients. Cover and heat through for 3 to 4 minutes. Remove whole cloves and discard. Stir lightly with a fork and serve immediately.

RED CABBAGE & APPLE SAUTÉ

This recipe from Canada Pork is a sure winner.

2 tbsp vegetable oil

1 medium onion, chopped

6 cups red cabbage,
  thinly sliced

1 tart apple, peeled,
  cored, and chopped

2 tbsp red wine vinegar

2 tbsp red currant or
  apple jelly

salt and pepper to taste

Heat oil in a large saucepan over medium-high heat. Add onion, and cook until softened but not brown. Add cabbage and cook, stirring frequently, until cabbage has softened but is still tender-crisp, about 10 minutes.

Add apple and cook another 2 to 3 minutes. Stir in vinegar, jelly, salt, and pepper. Cook, stirring constantly until jelly has dissolved and all ingredients are well combined.

CABBAGE ROLLS WITH APPLE-PAPRIKA SAUCE

From Lithuania, the home of my friend Antanina Fokaite.

CABBAGE ROLLS:

5 oz long-grain rice

1 1/2 cups chicken stock

1/8 tsp salt

1 tbsp salad oil

1 medium onion, chopped

1/2 lb bacon, diced

1/4 tsp garlic salt

1 tsp paprika

1/2 tsp caraway seeds

salt and pepper to taste

8 large cabbage leaves

APPLE-PAPRIKA SAUCE:

2 large tart apples, pared, cored, and thinly sliced

1/2 medium onion, chopped

1/2 tsp paprika

1 tsp salad oil

2 tbsp water

1 tbsp brown sugar

Cabbage Rolls: Cook rice in chicken broth and salt over medium heat, until tender, about 20 to 25 minutes. Preheat oven to 350°F. Heat oil, and sauté onion and bacon for 4 to 5 minutes. Sprinkle with garlic salt, paprika, caraway, salt, and pepper. Blanch cabbage leaves in boiling water for 3 minutes, one or two leaves at a time. Plunge into cold water immediately and dry well on paper towels. Combine rice with bacon mixture. Divide amongst cabbage leaves. Fold over leaves and make neat squares. Place on an oiled 9 x 13-inch cake pan. Bake for 30 minutes.

Sauce: Combine all ingredients in a saucepan. Cook over medium heat for 10 minutes, until apples and onion are soft. Serve hot over cabbage rolls.

SWEET POTATO CASSEROLE

4 large sweet potatoes, cooked, peeled, and sliced

1/4 cup granulated sugar

3/4 cup brown sugar

1/4 tsp salt

1/4 tsp cinnamon

4 tsp cornstarch

1 cup water

6 medium apples, pared, cored, and thinly sliced

2 tbsp butter

1/2 cup pecans, chopped

1 cup miniature marshmallows

Preheat oven to 350°F. Combine sugars, salt, cinnamon, cornstarch, and water in a saucepan. Cook over medium heat until boiling. Simmer about 2 to 3 minutes. Add apples and butter. Turn off heat. Put sweet potato slices in a casserole or baking dish. Spoon apple slices between and around potato slices. Sprinkle pecans throughout. Pour syrup over entire mixture. Bake in preheated oven approximately 50 minutes. Sprinkle with marshmallows, and bake another 5 to 10 minutes, until browned on top.

CLASSY APPLE SCALLOP

Serve this tasty dish as a hot relish with roast meats.

7–8 medium apples, pared, cored, and thinly sliced

1 tsp cinnamon

1/2 tsp nutmeg

1 tbsp lemon juice

1 cup all-purpose flour

1/2 cup brown sugar

1/2 cup butter or margarine

1 cup golden raisins

Preheat oven to 375°F. Butter 1 1/2-quart casserole dish. Combine apples, cinnamon, nutmeg, and lemon juice. Mix lightly to coat apples. Set aside. Combine flour and sugar. Cut in butter until mixture resembles coarse meal. Layer mixtures in casserole beginning with apples, then a sprinkle of the raisins, followed by the crumbs. Repeat layers. Bake for 30 minutes.

APPLE-TURNIP SCALLOP

1/4 cup butter, divided

1/2 cup onions, thinly sliced

3 cups turnip, pared and thinly sliced

1 1/2 cups apples, pared, cored, and sliced

2 tbsp flour

1 tsp granulated sugar

1 1/2 cups rich milk (1 cup 2% milk + 1/2 cup half and half)

Preheat oven to 350°F. Butter a 1 1/2-quart casserole dish. Melt 1 tbsp butter in a small pan and sauté onions until clear. Layer turnip, onion, and apples in casserole dish. Sprinkle each layer with a bit of flour and a light sprinkle of sugar. Dot mixture with remaining butter, and cover with milk. Cover casserole and bake for 30 minutes. Uncover and bake a further 30 minutes or until cooked.

APPLE & TOMATO SCALLOP

A low-cost family recipe handed down for several generations. From the kitchen of my aunt Winnifred Perry, one of Prince Edward Island's truly great cooks.

1 small onion, chopped

2 tbsp butter

1 1/2 cups soft bread-crumbs

2 1/2 cups stewed toma-toes (canned tomatoes may be used)

1 tbsp granulated sugar

salt and pepper to taste

2 medium tart apples, pared, cored, and sliced

Preheat oven to 350°F. Butter a 1-quart casserole dish. Sauté onion in butter until clear. Stir in bread crumbs and mix lightly to absorb the butter. In a medium bowl, combine remaining ingredients. Spread half in casserole. Then sprinkle with half of breadcrumb mixture. Repeat layers. Bake for 45 minutes.

SAUSAGE-STUFFED BAKED APPLES

Served with a tossed salad and whole wheat bread, these stuffed apples make a great supper.

1/4 cup butter or margarine

1 small onion, grated

1/2 lb sausage meat

1/2 cup soft breadcrumbs

1 tsp sage

1/8 tsp nutmeg

salt and pepper to taste

6–8 large apples, cored to within 1/2 inch of the base

2 tbsp lemon juice

1 tbsp beef bouillon powder

1 1/2 cups boiling water

Preheat oven to 400°F. Melt 2 tbsp of butter in a skillet. Sauté onion until clear, about 5 minutes. Remove onion from pan and set aside. Add remaining butter and cook sausage meat until evenly browned. Crumble meat with a fork. Using a slotted spoon, remove sausage from the pan and mix with onion. Stir in breadcrumbs, sage, nutmeg, salt, and pepper.

Widen the hole at the top of the apples, and cut one strip of peel around them to prevent bursting during baking time. Fill apples with stuffing mixture. Arrange in a greased baking dish. Combine lemon juice, beef bouillon, and boiling water. Pour around apples. Bake uncovered for 30 to 40 minutes, until apples are tender. Remove apples from baking dish. Serve immediately, using remaining liquid as a sauce.

APPLESAUCY BEETS

A colourful accompaniment to roast chicken.

6 medium beets, cooked, peeled, and chopped fine (use a food processor or potato masher)
....
1 cup applesauce
....
1 tbsp butter
....
salt and pepper to taste
....

Combine all ingredients in a saucepan. Heat until butter is melted and mixture is heated through. Serve immediately.

QUICK HARVARD BEETS

2/3 cup apple juice
....
1/2 cup cider vinegar
....
2 tbsp cornstarch
....
1 tbsp granulated sugar
....
1/2 tsp salt
....
3 cups beets, cooked and cubed
....

Combine apple juice, vinegar, cornstarch, sugar, and salt. Cook over medium heat until sauce is thick and clear. Fold in beets. Heat thoroughly. Serve hot.

SPICY APPLE GLAZE (FOR BAKED HAM)

Make your baked ham special with this easy glaze.

2/3 cup apple jelly

1/4 cup light corn syrup

1 tbsp cornstarch

1/3 cup apple juice

1/4 tsp cinnamon

Combine all ingredients. Cook, stirring constantly, until sauce is thickened. Brush over ham frequently during the last 15 to 20 minutes of baking.

Variations: For a fancy "special company dinner," top your ham with pineapple slices surrounded by maraschino cherries. Hold in place with toothpicks. Stud a few whole cloves around the fruit. Glaze with above mixture. Be sure to remove the toothpicks before taking your baked ham to the table. Your guests will say you're a gourmet.

FRIED APPLE RINGS

3 large baking apples, cored but not peeled

1/4 cup butter or margarine

1/4 cup granulated sugar

1/2 tsp cinnamon

Cut each apple into 3 or 4 thick slices. Heat butter in a heavy frying pan. Cook apple slices slowly in a single layer. Turn gently after 5 minutes, and cook other side for another 5 minutes. Apples should be lightly browned and tender. Place on a serving dish, and sprinkle with a combination of the sugar and cinnamon. Serve with pork.

DEEP-FRIED APPLE RINGS

1/2 cup all-purpose flour

1 tbsp granulated sugar

1 tsp baking powder

1/4 tsp salt

1 egg

1/3 cup milk

1 1/2 tsp vegetable oil

4 medium apples,
washed, cored, and
thinly sliced into rings

1 tbsp lemon juice

1/4 cup granulated sugar

fat for frying

1 tsp cinnamon

1 tbsp granulated sugar

Combine flour, sugar, baking powder, and salt. Beat egg, milk, and oil in a separate dish. Combine the 2 mixtures and beat until smooth. The mixture will be much like pancake batter.

Sprinkle apple slices with lemon juice. Toss in 1/4 cup sugar. Heat fat to 375°F. Dip apple rings in batter and cook in fat for 4 minutes, turning once to brown rings on both sides. Sprinkle rings with a mixture of 1 tbsp sugar and 1 tsp cinnamon while still warm. Serve with roast meats.

AUNT WINNIE'S SPICY APPLE MUFFINS

Muffins are not just for breakfast. Impress your guests with hot muffins for an evening snack.

2 cups all-purpose flour

1/3 cup granulated sugar

1 tbsp baking powder

1 tsp cinnamon

1/2 tsp salt

1/4 tsp nutmeg

1 large apple, pared and grated

1 egg, well beaten

1 cup milk

1/4 cup margarine, melted

Preheat oven to 400°F. Grease 18 medium muffin cups. Sift flour, sugar, baking powder, cinnamon, salt, and nutmeg into a mixing bowl. Add grated apple. Toss lightly. Combine egg, milk, and margarine. Add to flour mixture. Stir only until moistened. Batter will be lumpy. Spoon into prepared muffin tins to 2/3 full. Bake 20 to 25 minutes. Serve hot.

APPLE TURNOVERS

Make your favourite tea biscuit recipe. Roll dough to 1/4-inch thick and cut into 4-inch squares. Place 1 tbsp thickened, sweetened applesauce on each square. Fold diagonally in half, and bake as biscuit recipe states. If more flavour is desired, add cinnamon or honey to applesauce, or substitute apple jelly, marmalade, or apple butter. While turnovers are hot, you might like to drizzle them with a combination of icing sugar and warm water.

CINNAMON-APPLE PINWHEELS

BISCUIT BASE:

2 cups all-purpose flour

1 1/2 tsp baking powder

1 tsp salt

1/2 tsp baking soda

1/3 cup margarine

3/4 cup sour milk or
  buttermilk

FILLING:

1 1/2 cups apples, pared,
  cored, and finely
  chopped

1/2 cup sugar

1 tsp cinnamon

Base: Preheat oven to 450°F. Grease a cookie sheet. Sift flour, baking powder, salt, and baking soda into a medium bowl. Cut in margarine until mixture resembles coarse meal. Stir in sour milk until dough sticks together. Gently form dough into a ball and knead very lightly on a floured surface. Roll to 1/4-inch thickness.

Filling: Combine apples, sugar, and cinnamon. Spread over dough. Roll as if for jelly roll. Slice into 1-inch thicknesses. Place on prepared cookie sheet. Bake 12 to 15 minutes. Serve with butter, or if glaze is desired, with a mixture of icing sugar and warm milk.

APPLE DOUGHNUTS

This recipe is included by special request of Muriel Bell of Searletown, a talented Island cook and a lover of doughnuts.

2 tbsp vegetable oil

1/2 cup granulated sugar

1/2 cup brown sugar

2 eggs

1/4 cup milk

1/2 tsp vanilla

1 cup applesauce, unsweetened

2 1/4 cups all-purpose flour

1 1/2 tsp baking powder

1/2 tsp baking soda

1/2 tsp cinnamon

1/2 tsp nutmeg

1/4 tsp salt

1/4 tsp cloves

oil for frying

cinnamon sugar (optional)

Combine oil, granulated sugar, brown sugar, and eggs, and beat until light. Beat in milk, vanilla, and applesauce. Sift flour, baking powder, baking soda, cinnamon, nutmeg, salt, and cloves. Add to first mixture. Stir until thoroughly moistened. Heat about 3 to 4 inches of oil in a deep pot or electric fryer, to 360°F. Drop batter by rounded teaspoonfuls or with a doughnut press. Cook only a few doughnuts at a time. Fry for 2 to 3 minutes, turning once. Drain on paper towels or brown paper.

Cinnamon sugar: In a paper bag, combine 1/2 cup granulated sugar with 1/2 to 1 tsp cinnamon. Shake hot doughnuts in this mixture.

PASTRY AND PIES

Remember the pies Grandmother used to make? Was apple pie your favourite? Apple pie is the most popular dessert in North America, and there's more variety in apple than in any other type of pie. I've tried to include a good cross-section of North American favourites, as well as apple pies from around the world. In these pages you'll find everything from basic apple pies to a mincemeat pie (a dessert once thought to be "unholy"), along with easy-to-prepare pastry recipes. Follow the directions carefully and everyone will applaud your perfect pies.

Pastry-making Hints

Those who feel less than confident at pastry making will find recipes here that are flaky and tender every time. The secrets to pastry making are simple: a light hand and cool ingredients. Rub the fat into the flour gently, using a pastry blender, two knives, or the tips of your fingers. Lift the mixture up as you blend it, to trap as much air as possible into the ingredients. (I like to use a food processor to mix the flour and fat, mixing small portions at a time. This adds air and makes a very light pastry.)

Add liquids that are nearly ice cold. Mix lightly with a fork until the pastry is just holding together. After liquid is added, handle pastry as little as possible. Over-handling and excess flour will cause tough pastry. If your pastry is sticky, chill in the refrigerator before rolling.

DOUBLE-CRUST PASTRY

Makes enough for one (9-inch) double-crust pie.

2 cups all-purpose flour

1 tsp salt

3/4 cup shortening

5–6 tbsp cold water

Combine flour and salt. Cut in shortening until mixture resembles coarse meal. Add water, a little at a time, mixing lightly with a fork. Shape dough into a ball. Divide into 2 portions, and roll out on a lightly floured surface, to 1/8-inch thickness. Place loosely in pie pan. Bake as directed in pie recipe.

PERFECT PASTRY

I copied this recipe from a television cooking show over twenty years ago and it's still my favourite. The recipe makes enough for 3 to 4 double-crust pies.

5 cups all-purpose flour

1 tsp salt

1 tbsp sugar

1/4 tsp baking soda

1 lb lard

1 egg

1 tbsp lemon juice
 or vinegar

cold water

Combine flour and lard with a pastry blender until mixture resembles coarse meal. Sprinkle with salt and toss lightly with a fork. Beat egg in a measuring cup. Add lemon juice, and enough cold water to make 1 cup of liquid. Add to flour mixture, and mix lightly with a fork, until pastry is just holding together. Divide and roll on a lightly floured board. If you have any leftover pastry, simply seal in plastic wrap and freeze. Thaw at room temperature or in the refrigerator when ready to use.

NEVER-FAIL PASTRY

5 cups all-purpose flour

1 tbsp salt

1 tbsp granulated sugar

1 lb shortening

1 large egg

cold water

Sift flour, salt, and sugar. Cut in shortening with a pastry blender. Beat egg in a measuring cup. Add water to make 1 cup. Mix liquid lightly into flour mixture with a fork. Knead very slightly. Roll on a lightly floured board, or seal in airtight wrap and place in refrigerator until ready to use.

BEST-EVER PASTRY (FOR FRUIT PIES)

5 1/2 cups all-purpose flour

1 1/2 tsp salt

1 tsp baking powder

3 tbsp brown sugar

1 lb lard or shortening

1 egg

1 tbsp vinegar

cold water

Combine flour, salt, baking powder, and sugar. Cut in lard or shortening, until mixture resembles coarse meal. Break egg into measuring cup and add vinegar. Beat with a fork. Add water to make 3/4 cup liquid. Gradually blend into flour mixture, mixing with a fork. Add only enough liquid to make dough cling together. Divide and roll on a lightly floured board. Makes enough pastry for 3 double-crust pies.

BASIC APPLE PIE

pastry for 9-inch
double-crust pie

6 cups apples, peeled,
cored, and sliced

1 cup granulated sugar
(more or less depending
on tartness of apples)

1/4 tsp nutmeg

1 tsp lemon juice

1 tbsp butter

Preheat oven to 450°F. Line pie plate with pastry. Put apples in a large bowl, sprinkle with sugar and nutmeg. Spread in pie plate. Sprinkle with lemon juice and dot with butter. Cover with remaining crust. Bake for 10 minutes, reduce heat to 375°F, and continue baking until apples are tender and pastry is nicely browned.

SUGAR-DUSTED APPLE PIE

Of the dozens of apple pie recipes I've found, this is perhaps the easiest and best loved of them all.

pastry for 9-inch
double-crust pie

6 cups apples, peeled,
cored, and sliced

2 tbsp all-purpose flour

3/4 to 1 cup granulated
sugar

3/4 tsp cinnamon

1/8 tsp nutmeg

2 tbsp butter

Preheat oven to 400°F. Line pie plate with pastry. Combine apples, flour, sugar, cinnamon, and nutmeg. Cover pastry with apple mixture. Dot with butter and top with remaining pastry. Cut steam vents in top of pastry. Sprinkle with granulated sugar, if desired. Bake for 45 to 50 minutes.

SOUTHERN APPLE PIE

Orange juice and nutmeg make a delicious difference in this one-crust pie.

pastry for 9-inch
single-crust pie

6 cups apples, peeled,
cored, and sliced

3/4 cup granulated sugar

2 tbsp tapioca starch

1/2 tsp nutmeg

juice of small orange

Preheat oven to 400°F. Line pie plate with pastry. Combine apples, sugar, starch, nutmeg, and orange juice. Spread in pie plate. Dot with butter. Bake for 10 minutes, reduce heat to 375°F, and bake a further 30 to 40 minutes, until apples are tender.

APPLE & CREAM PIE

pastry for 9-inch
double-crust pie

6–7 cups apples, peeled,
cored, and sliced

1 cup granulated sugar

1 tsp cinnamon

1/2 cup raisins

2 tbsp butter

1/2 cup whipping cream

Preheat oven to 425°F. Line pie plate with half the pastry. Combine apples, sugar, cinnamon, and raisins. Spread in pie pan. Dot with butter. Cover with remaining pastry and cut slits in top to vent steam. Bake for 50 minutes. Remove from oven and pour whipping cream through the top vent in crust. Return to oven and bake 5 minutes longer.

DUTCH APPLE PIE

pastry for 9-inch
    single-crust pie

6 cups apples, peeled,
    cored, and sliced

1 1/4 cups brown sugar

1/2 cup all-purpose flour

1 tsp cinnamon

1/3 cup butter or
    margarine

1/4 cup whipping cream

Preheat oven to 425°F. Combine sugar, flour, cinnamon, and butter until crumbly. Spread 1/3 of mixture on pie shell, cover with apples, and sprinkle remaining mixture over apples. Pour cream on top. Bake 15 minutes. Reduce heat to 350°F and bake 30 minutes longer, until apples are tender. Serve warm or cold.

APPLE-CARAMEL PIE

pastry for 9-inch
    deep-dish pie shell

6 cups apples, peeled,
    cored, and sliced

1 1/2 cups brown sugar

1/2 cup butter

1/2 cup all-purpose flour

shake of salt

2 tsp cinnamon

1/2 cup walnuts, chopped

Preheat oven to 350°F. Line pie pan with pastry. Arrange apple slices over pastry. Combine brown sugar, butter, flour, salt, and cinnamon. Spread over apples; sprinkle with walnuts. Bake 50 minutes. Serve with whipped cream or ice cream.

DOWN UNDER PIE

For many years I've had penpals in Australia and New Zealand. Granny Smith apples first came from New Zealand, and are featured in this pie from the land down under.

PASTRY:

1 cup all-purpose flour

1 tbsp granulated sugar

1/3 cup butter

4 tbsp cold water

FILLING:

4 cups Granny Smith apples, peeled, cored, and sliced

2 eggs

2/3 cup cream

1/3 cup granulated sugar

1 tsp vanilla

1/2 cup apricot preserves

Pastry: Preheat oven to 400°F. Combine flour, sugar, and butter until crumbly. Mix in water until moistened. Roll out on lightly floured board. Spread in a 10-inch pie pan. Prick pastry with a fork, cover with tin foil, and bake for 10 minutes. Remove from oven and cool crust.

Filling: Reduce oven temperature to 350°F. Arrange apples over crust in decorative pattern. Beat eggs, cream, sugar, and vanilla. Pour over apples. Bake for 45 minutes, until lightly browned and custard is firm. Cool slightly in pan. Melt apricot jam and brush over apples. Cool to room temperature and serve.

DOWN UNDER APPLE TART

You guessed it: this lovely apple pie comes from Australia.

pastry for 8-inch pie shell

1/3 cup brown sugar

1/4 cup butter

1 tbsp lemon juice

1 tbsp corn syrup

2 large apples

Preheat oven to 400°F. Place sugar and butter in a Pyrex or glass pie plate. Put in oven until butter is melted. Add lemon juice and corn syrup. Arrange apple slices in a circular pattern over sugar mixture. Cover with pastry, tucking in around the edges. Bake 30 to 35 minutes. Remove from oven and cool for 5 minutes. Invert tart onto a serving plate. Serve with ice cream.

SOUR CREAM–APPLE PIE

PIE:

pastry for 9-inch
  single-crust pie

2 cups apples, peeled,
  cored, and thinly sliced

2 tbsp all-purpose flour

3/4 cup granulated sugar

1/4 tsp salt

1/4 tsp nutmeg

1 egg

1 cup sour cream

1 tsp vanilla

TOPPING:

1/2 cup granulated sugar

1/3 cup all-purpose flour

1 tsp cinnamon

1/4 cup butter, melted

Pie: Preheat oven to 400°F. Place pastry in pie plate. Combine apples, flour, sugar, salt, nutmeg, egg, sour cream, and vanilla. Spread over pastry. Bake for 15 minutes. Reduce heat to 350°F and bake 30 minutes longer.

Topping: Combine sugar, flour, cinnamon, and butter, and sprinkle over apple mixture. Bake 10 minutes to brown top.

APPLE BUTTER–PUMPKIN PIE

pastry for 9-inch pie shell

2 cups pumpkin purée

1 cup Apple Butter (see page 213 for recipe)

1/2 cup brown sugar

1 tsp cinnamon

1/2 tsp ginger

1/2 tsp nutmeg

pinch of salt

1 1/2 cups milk, scalded

3 large eggs, beaten

Preheat oven to 400°F. Line pie pan with pastry. Combine remaining ingredients in a large bowl. Mix well. Pour into unbaked pie shell. Bake 10 minutes. Reduce heat to 325°F and bake 40 to 45 minutes, until knife inserted in centre of pie comes out clean.

CRUNCHY APPLE-BANANA PIE

pastry for 9-inch pie shell

3 medium apples, peeled, cored, and sliced

2 bananas, peeled and sliced

2 tbsp lemon juice

1 cup all-purpose flour

1/2 cup brown sugar

1/2 cup granulated sugar

1/2 tsp cinnamon

1/2 tsp nutmeg

1/2 cup margarine, softened

Preheat oven to 400°F. Line pie pan with pastry. Combine apples, bananas, and lemon juice. Let stand while mixing other ingredients. Combine flour, sugars, spices, and margarine until mixture resembles coarse meal. Sprinkle over fruit mixture. Bake 35 to 45 minutes. Cover pie with foil if it begins to brown too quickly.

SNOW-TOPPED APPLE PIE

PIE:

pastry for 9-inch
  single-crust pie

7 cups apples, peeled,
  cored, and sliced

3/4 cup maple syrup

1/4 cup water

2 tbsp butter or
  margarine, melted

1/4 cup all-purpose flour

TOPPING:

1 cup cream cheese

1 1/2 cups icing sugar

2–3 tbsp milk

1 tsp vanilla

unpeeled apple wedges,
  for garnish

lemon juice

Pie: Preheat oven to 425°F. Line pie plate with pastry. Trim, and prick with a fork. Bake 10 to 12 minutes. Remove from oven and cool. In a saucepan, combine apples, maple syrup, and water. Bring to a boil. Cover and simmer until apples are tender (about 10 minutes). Stir occasionally. Drain and reserve syrup. In the same saucepan, combine melted butter and flour. Add syrup, and cook over medium heat, stirring constantly until thickened. Pour over apples. Spread mixture in pie shell.

Topping: Combine cream cheese, icing sugar, milk, and vanilla in a mixing bowl. Beat with rotary beater or electric mixer until light and fluffy. Swirl onto cooled pie, and garnish with unpeeled apple wedges dipped in lemon juice.

WINTER-FRUIT PIE

A Christmas treat that's colourful as well as delicious.

pastry for 9-inch
double-crust pie

2 cups apples, peeled,
cored, and chopped

2 cups cranberries,
chopped

1/2 cup water

1/2 cup granulated sugar

2 tbsp flour

1/2 cup corn syrup

dash of salt

1/2 tsp orange rind

Combine apples, cranberries, water, sugar, flour, corn syrup, salt, and orange rind in a saucepan. Cook until thickened. Preheat oven to 425°F. Line pie pan with half pastry. Cover with pie filling, and top with remaining pastry in a lattice-topped design. Bake 35 to 45 minutes. Serve with ice cream.

APPLE-PEAR PIE

pastry for 9-inch
double-crust pie

3 cups apples, peeled
and sliced

3 cups pears, peeled
and sliced

1/2 cup granulated sugar

3 tbsp cornstarch

1 tsp cinnamon

1/4 tsp nutmeg

2 tbsp butter

Preheat oven to 400°F. Roll out half pastry and line a 9-inch pie plate. Combine apples, pears, sugar, cornstarch, cinnamon, and nutmeg. Toss to mix. Pour into pastry-lined pan. Dot with butter. Cover with remaining pastry. Cut steam vents in top crust. Bake 40 to 45 minutes. Cool on wire rack until serving time. This pie may be served hot or cool, with ice cream, whipped cream, or cheddar cheese.

CREAMY APPLE-CUSTARD PIE

pastry for 9-inch
single-crust pie

6 cups apples, peeled,
cored, and sliced

3/4 cup granulated sugar

1/4 cup all-purpose flour

3/4 tsp cinnamon

1/4 tsp salt

1 1/4 cups whipping
cream

2 eggs

1/4 tsp vanilla

Preheat oven to 400°F. Line pie plate with pastry, prick with fork, and bake for 10 minutes. Combine apples, sugar, flour, cinnamon, and salt; toss together to mix. Arrange on pie shell in a decorative pattern. Blend cream, eggs, and vanilla thoroughly and pour over apples. Return to oven and bake for 30 minutes. Reduce heat to 300°F and continue cooking until custard is set. Serve warm.

MOCK MINCE PIE FILLING

Don't let the list of ingredients fool you. For a quick homemade mince pie, this recipe from the kitchen of my mother-in-law, Elizabeth Reeves, cannot be beat. One of the reasons I like this recipe is because it uses up any dry bread I might have, so I often double or triple the ingredients.

3 large apples, peeled, cored, and sliced

water

1 cup breadcrumbs

2 cups hot water

1 cup molasses

1 cup granulated sugar

1 cup seeded raisins

2 eggs

1 tsp salt

1 tsp cinnamon

1/2 tsp cloves

1 tsp vinegar

Put apples and a very small amount of water in a heavy saucepan. Cook on low heat until apples are warm. Add all remaining ingredients and simmer for approximately 1 hour. Cooking time will be a bit longer if you double or triple the recipe.

APPLE CRUMB CRUNCH PIE

PIE:

pastry for 9-inch
  single-crust pie

5 cups apples, peeled,
  cored, and sliced

3/4 cup granulated sugar

1/2 tsp cinnamon

1/4 tsp salt

2 tbsp all-purpose flour

1/4 cup water

1 tsp lemon juice

1 tbsp butter

CRUMB TOPPING:

1 tbsp butter

1 tbsp granulated sugar

3 tbsp all-purpose flour

1/4 tsp salt

Pie: Preheat oven to 425°F. Line pie pan with pastry. Combine apples, sugar, cinnamon, salt, flour, water, and lemon juice. Spread over pastry. Dot with butter.

Topping: Combine all ingredients and sprinkle over apples. Bake in preheated oven for 45 to 50 minutes.

Variation #1: Omit topping and bake as a double-crust pie. Sprinkle apples with 1/4 tsp nutmeg. Bake as directed.

Variation #2: Omit lemon juice, nutmeg, and water. Add 1/2 cup cream. Bake as a double-crust pie.

APPLE TORTE

Joan Bonk of Toronto, Ontario, sent me this delicious recipe several years ago. It's well worth the little extra effort it requires.

PASTRY LAYER:

1/2 cup butter or margarine

1/3 cup granulated sugar

1/4 tsp vanilla

1 cup all-purpose flour

FILLING LAYER:

1 cup cream cheese, softened

1/4 cup granulated sugar

1 egg, beaten

1/2 tsp vanilla

TOPPING:

1/3 cup granulated sugar

1/2 tsp cinnamon

4 cups apples, peeled, cored, and sliced

1/3 cup almonds, blanched and sliced

Pastry: Preheat oven to 450°F. To prepare pastry layer: Cream butter, sugar, and vanilla. Blend in flour. Spread pastry on bottom and sides of 9-inch springform pan.

Filling: Combine cream cheese and sugar in mixer bowl. Beat at high speed until well mixed. Blend in beaten egg and vanilla until mixture is smooth. Pour into pastry-lined pan.

Topping: Combine sugar and cinnamon. Sprinkle mixture over apples, and toss to mix. Arrange apples over cream cheese layer. Sprinkle with almonds.

Bake for 10 minutes. Reduce heat to 400°F and continue cooking for 25 to 30 minutes. Place on a wire rack; loosen rim of pan. Cool completely, cover, and refrigerate or freeze.

CRAN-APPLE PIE

Cranberries and apples combine well in a variety of recipes. Here they team up for pie that's a real treat. Serve this pie when still slightly warm, with vanilla ice cream.

pastry for 9-inch
  double-crust pie

6 cups apples, peeled,
  cored, and sliced

1 cup cranberries

1/2 cup walnuts, finely
  chopped

3/4 cup brown sugar,
  firmly packed

2 tbsp all-purpose flour

1/2 tsp cinnamon

1/2 tsp nutmeg

2 tbsp butter

1 egg, beaten with
  1 tbsp water

granulated sugar

Preheat oven to 425°F. Line pie pan with half pastry. Combine apples, cranberries, walnuts, sugar, flour, cinnamon, and nutmeg in a large bowl. Toss to lightly mix. Put into pastry-lined pie pan. Dot with butter. Cover with remaining pastry. Cut slits in top of pastry for steam to escape. Brush top of pastry with mixture of beaten egg and water. Sprinkle with granulated sugar. Bake for 12 minutes, reduce heat to 350°F, and continue cooking for 45 minutes or until pastry is golden brown. Cool until slightly warm, and serve with ice cream.

SWEDISH APPLE FLAN

A tasty apple flan glazed with apricot preserves, from the kitchen of Inga-Lill Harding.

PASTRY:

1 cup all-purpose flour

1 tbsp granulated sugar

1/4 tsp salt

1/2 cup butter

2 tbsp ice water

FILLING:

3 medium tart apples,
   pared, cored, and
   thinly sliced

2 tbsp lemon juice

2 tbsp granulated sugar

1 tsp beaten egg

2 tbsp butter

GLAZE:

1/2 cup apricot preserves

Pastry: Combine flour, 1 tbsp granulated sugar, salt, and 1/2 cup butter. Cut with a pastry blender or 2 knives until mixture resembles coarse meal. Sprinkle with ice water, and mix lightly. Form into a flat, round ball about 6 inches in diameter. Wrap, and chill in refrigerator until firm enough to roll, about 2 hours.

Filling: Toss apples in lemon juice and 2 tbsp sugar. Set aside.

Preheat oven to 400°F. Roll pastry on a lightly floured board to approximately 1/8-inch thickness. Place in a 9-inch round flan dish or layer cake pan. Trim edges of pastry and reserve trimmings. Prick pastry with a fork. Bake for 15 minutes. Cool on cookie sheet on top of a wire rack. Arrange apples in overlapping slices around flan, leaving 1/2 inch of outer edge uncovered. Hand roll remaining pastry into a rope long enough to circle edge of pan. Press around crust. Brush with beaten egg. Melt butter and drizzle over apples, along with any lemon juice left in apple bowl. Bake for 20 minutes, until apples are tender.

Glaze: Remove from oven and glaze with apricot preserves. Return to oven and bake until preserves are melted, about 5 minutes. Cool on a cookie sheet or a wire rack for 10 minutes. Loosen with a spatula and slide out onto rack. Serve warm or at room temperature.

PRESERVES

Preserving, at its simplest, is the act of "putting by" in times of plenty, so that there are wholesome foods available in times of need. I have found that there is nothing more satisfying than filling the storage cupboard with homemade preserves. Since the early Romans dropped whole apples in pots of honey, cooks through the centuries have been "putting by" an abundance of apples.

Apples can be savoured in jams, relishes, chutneys, pie fillings, and tasty apple preserves. In this chapter, you will learn a variety of safe techniques and recipes for preserving apples. One word of advice: preserves need to mellow for a month for maximum flavour, so resist the temptation to sample too early.

Pressure Canning Preserves

Moulds, yeast, enzymes, and bacteria are food agents that can cause spoilage in preserves. Of these four, moulds, enzymes, and yeast can be destroyed by boiling at 212°F (100°C). The more dangerous bacteria, especially bacteria that cause botulism, can only be destroyed by a temperature of 240°F (115°C).

In pressure canning, after some of the water is converted to steam and air is exhausted from the canner through a vent pipe, a pressure regulator is put over the vent pipe, and pressure from the steam builds up within the canner. As the pressure builds to the desired level, the regulator will begin to rock. Cooking time is measured from this "rocking point."

A 5-pound pressure regulator will raise the water temperature to 228°F (110°C). A 10-pound pressure regulator will raise the water temperature to 240°F (115°C). A 15-pound pressure regulator will raise water temperature to 250°F (120°C).

Carefully follow the manufacturer's instructions for using your pressure canner. And if, after pressure canning or boiling, food does not look or smell right, always discard it without tasting.

MINCEMEAT PIE FILLING

This recipe is from the kitchen of my niece Christina Klarenbeek. It can be prepared when apples are plentiful and stored for later use.

2 lbs lean boneless beef, coarsely ground

1/2 lb suet, coarsely ground

2 oranges

12 cups tart apples, peeled, cored, and coarsely chopped

2 1/2 cups dark sultana raisins

2 1/2 cups golden raisins

1 1/2 cups candied citron peel, chopped

4 cups brown sugar

1 tbsp salt

1 tbsp cinnamon

1 tbsp allspice

1 tsp cloves

1 tsp nutmeg

4 cups apple cider

1 cup brandy

In a large cooking pot, combine ground beef and suet. Grate peel from oranges and set aside. Remove all white membrane from oranges, chop orange sections, and add to meat mixture. Stir in apples, raisins, peel, sugar, salt, spices, and apple cider. Mix well. Bring to a boil over medium heat, and reduce to low. Simmer uncovered for 15 to 20 minutes. Stir in brandy. Ladle into sterilized jars, leaving 1-inch headspace. Can, with pressure at 10 pounds for 20 minutes, following manufacturer's instructions.

Note: Brandy may be replaced with 1 cup apple juice or cider and 1 tbsp brandy extract. If you use the replacement, add it before bringing the mixture to a boil.

PRESERVED APPLE PIE FILLING

Another recipe from the kitchen of Christina Klarenbeek, who says she prefers Granny Smith or a mixture of McIntosh and Spys for this pie filling. Experiment with apple varieties that appeal to your personal tastes—I tested this recipe with a mixture of unknown apples that I found growing on a farm lane, and had excellent results.

approx 15 cups firm apples, pared, cored, and sliced (6 lbs of prepared fruit, altogether)

2 cups granulated sugar

1/2 cup quick-cooking tapioca

2 tbsp cinnamon

1 tbsp nutmeg

1/4 cup grated lemon rind

juice of 1/2 lemon

Put apple slices in a solution of salt and water, or an antioxidant. If the latter is used, follow package directions to prevent darkening. Combine sugar, tapioca, cinnamon, and nutmeg. Rinse apples in clear, cold water. Drain apples and sprinkle with sugar mixture. Let sit for 30 minutes. Add lemon peel and juice. Cover. Cook over medium heat to 212°F. Ladle into sterilized jars, leaving 1-inch headspace. Process in boiling water bath for 20 minutes. Yields 6 to 7 pints.

APPLE-TOMATO MINCEMEAT

From the kitchen of Brenda Rogers of Linkletter, PEI.

13 cups apples, cored and chopped

13 cups green tomatoes, chopped

3 lbs brown sugar

1 lb currants

1 lb sultana raisins

1 tsp cinnamon

1 tsp cloves

1 tsp allspice

1 tsp salt

2 tbsp vinegar or lemon juice

Combine all ingredients in a large saucepan. Simmer over medium-low heat for 3 hours. Bottle and seal in sterilized jars.

GREEN TOMATO MINCEMEAT

This recipe has been used for several generations in our family as a pie filling and in cookies and squares, or heated as a sundae topping. The recipe was given to me by Muriel Bell of Searletown, PEI.

15 medium green
tomatoes, chopped
(about 8 cups)

15 medium apples, cored
and chopped
(about 8 cups)

1 lb seedless raisins

1 lb seeded raisins

4 1/2 cups brown sugar

1 tsp cinnamon

1 tsp cloves

1 tsp salt

1 tbsp vinegar

3 tbsp butter

Combine all ingredients in a large pot and heat over medium heat to a simmer. Simmer uncovered for 2 hours, stirring occasionally. Remove from heat. Bottle and seal immediately.

APPLE CHUTNEY

8 medium apples, pared,
cored, and chopped

2 cups sultana raisins

grated peel of 2 oranges

4 1/2 cups granulated
sugar

1/2 cup white vinegar

2 tbsp whole cloves, tied
in a cheesecloth bag

Combine all ingredients in a heavy saucepan. Bring to a rolling boil, reduce heat, and cook slowly on simmer until apples are tender. Pour into hot sterilized bottles and seal immediately.

APPLE-ZUCCHINI CHUTNEY

6 cups apples, peeled, cored, and chopped

6 cups zucchini, chopped

2 cups onions, finely chopped

1 cup prunes, stoned and chopped

1/2 cup candied ginger, chopped

2 cups sultana raisins

2 cups crushed pineapple

3 1/2 cups brown sugar

1 1/2 cups cider vinegar

1 tbsp cinnamon

2 tsp allspice

2 tsp salt

1 tsp cloves

1 tsp mustard seeds

Combine all ingredients in a large pot. Bring to a boil over medium heat and simmer until thickened, about 1 1/2 to 2 hours. Stir often to prevent sticking. Pour into hot sterilized jars and seal at once.

APPLE-TOMATO CHUTNEY

A moderately hot chutney that tastes great with roast beef or pork.

6 cups tart apples, pared, cored, and chopped

10 cups ripe tomatoes, peeled and chopped

2 1/2 cups seedless raisins

2 1/2 cups dark brown sugar, packed

1 tbsp salt

1 tbsp cinnamon

1 tsp garlic salt

1 tsp allspice

1/2 tsp ginger

1/2 tsp cloves

2 cups cider vinegar

Combine all ingredients in a large cooking pot. Place over medium heat and bring to boiling point, stirring constantly. Cover, reduce heat, and simmer for 10 minutes. Uncover and simmer until thick, about 30 to 40 minutes longer. Stir often, as this mixture can easily stick to the pot. Ladle into sterilized jars. Seal immediately. Process in boiling water bath for 10 minutes.

PEACHY APPLE CHUTNEY

A tangy combo of fruits and spices that is delicious with roast meats, barbecues, and cold cuts. You can also serve this chutney on crackers with cream cheese, as an hors d'oeuvre.

3 cups tart apples, peeled, cored, and chopped

3 cups peaches, peeled and chopped

1 cup green pepper, chopped

1 small onion, chopped

3 1/2 cups stewed tomatoes

1 tsp salt

1/2 tsp ginger

1/2 tsp dry mustard

1/2 cup white wine vinegar

3/4 cup liquid honey

Combine apples, peaches, pepper, onion, tomatoes, salt, ginger, mustard, and vinegar in a heavy saucepan. Bring to a rolling boil, stirring often. Reduce heat and cook for 30 minutes, stirring often to prevent sticking. Stir in honey and cook for a further 30 minutes. Ladle into hot sterilized jars and seal immediately.

Note: For a different dressing on a tossed salad, combine Peachy Apple Chutney with mayonnaise, adding chutney to taste.

WALK-IN-THE-GARDEN RELISH

This all-purpose relish uses up the leftovers when you've almost finished your fall preserving. You'll want to plan ahead for this recipe—the vegetables must sit overnight.

2 cups apples, peeled and coarsely ground

2 cups green tomatoes, coarsely ground

2 cups cucumbers, peeled, seeded, and coarsely ground

2 cups onions, peeled and finely chopped

1 green pepper, seeded and chopped

1 red pepper, seeded and chopped

4 tsp salt

5 cups cold water

1 1/2 cups cider vinegar

2 cups granulated sugar

1 tbsp mustard seed

1/2 cup all-purpose flour

1 tbsp dry mustard

1/2 cup cider vinegar

Combine apples, green tomatoes, cucumbers, onions, green pepper, and red pepper with salt and water. Let sit overnight. Then drain thoroughly and mix with 1 1/2 cups vinegar, sugar, and mustard seed. Bring to a boil over medium-low heat and cook slowly for 30 minutes. Stir often to prevent sticking. Combine flour, dry mustard, and 1/2 cup vinegar to make a paste. Stir into vegetable and fruit mixture. Simmer another 30 minutes until thick and cooked through. Ladle into hot sterilized jars, leaving a 1-inch headspace. Process in boiling water bath for 10 minutes.

AUNT MARTHA'S RELISH

This recipe comes from a lady who took me under her wing when I was a young married woman, making me feel at home in a new community. Our children remember her fondly as the lady who always gave them "a cookie for each hand." The late Martha Burns was a great cook, as this colourful relish will testify. Prepare ahead for this recipe, as some ingredients must sit overnight.

5 cups cucumbers, peeled

10 cups onions, peeled

2 tbsp salt

cold water

1 bunch celery

3 sweet red peppers

2 large apples

5 cups white vinegar

8 cups brown sugar

2 tbsp mustard seed

1 tbsp turmeric

2/3 cup all-purpose flour

1/2 cup dry mustard

Finely chop cucumbers and onions, using a food chopper. Cover with a mixture of 2 tbsp salt and cold water. Let sit overnight in brine. Drain thoroughly in morning and rinse with cold water. Put celery, peppers, and apples through chopper, chopping finely, and add to other vegetables. Put mustard seed in a small cheesecloth bag and add to vegetable and fruit mixture. Stir in vinegar and bring to a boil over medium heat. Combine flour, dry mustard, and turmeric. Add to vegetables and simmer for 30 minutes, until thickened. Ladle into sterilized jars and seal immediately.

KING EDWARD RELISH

8 large apples, peeled and cored

8 cucumbers, seeded

3 sweet red peppers

3 sweet green peppers

1/4 cup pickling salt

6 large onions, peeled

2 heads celery, diced fine

1 tbsp mustard seed

3 tbsp dry mustard

1/4 cup all-purpose flour

3 cups granulated sugar

1 tbsp celery seed

1 tbsp turmeric

4 cups cider vinegar

Put apples, cucumbers, peppers, and onions through a food chopper. Sprinkle with pickling salt and let stand overnight. Drain in morning and rinse thoroughly with cold water. Add celery to vegetable mixture. Combine mustard seed, dry mustard, flour, sugar, celery seed, and vinegar in a large pot. Cook over medium heat until thickened. Add vegetables and bring to a boil. Simmer until thickened. Bottle and seal immediately.

APPLE-BEET RELISH

A beautiful deep-red relish that's easy to prepare.

6 large apples, peeled, cored, and finely chopped

6 cups beets, cooked, peeled, and chopped

2 large onions, peeled and finely chopped

1 1/2 cups granulated sugar

1 1/2 cups white vinegar

1/2 cup water

1 (4-inch) stick cinnamon (broken and tied in a cheesecloth bag)

1 tbsp salt

Combine all ingredients in a heavy pot. Cover. Simmer for 20 minutes, stirring often. Remove from heat. Remove cinnamon stick. Bottle and seal immediately.

Variation: For a slightly richer taste, try making this relish with 1 2/3 cups brown sugar instead of using granulated sugar. Brown sugar combines well with both apples and beets.

APPLE-RASPBERRY CONSERVE

2 cups water

8 cups granulated sugar

6 cups apples, peeled, cored, and chopped

3 cups red or black raspberries

Boil sugar and water until temperature reaches 230°F on a candy thermometer. Add apples and cook 2 minutes. Add raspberries and cook 10 minutes longer. Ladle into sterilized bottles and seal immediately.

THREE-FRUIT JAM

Apples, pears, and cranberry combine with cinnamon for a spicy jam that's beyond compare.

8 medium tart apples, peeled and cored

8 pears, peeled and cored

1 1/2 cups cranberries

4 cups granulated sugar

1/2 tsp cinnamon

juice of 1 lemon

Put apples, pears, and cranberries through a food chopper or blender. Add sugar, cinnamon, and lemon juice. Bring to a boil slowly, over medium heat. Simmer until mixture thickens, removing any scum from mixture as it forms. Total cooking time will be approximately 1 hour. Ladle into hot sterilized jars and seal immediately.

TOMATO-APPLE JAM

8 cups ripe tomatoes,
   peeled and chopped

3 cups tart apples,
   peeled, cored, and
   chopped

1 large lemon, sliced

4 cups granulated sugar

Combine tomatoes, apples, and lemon in a heavy pot. Heat to simmering. Stir in sugar, and continue to simmer for 1 1/2 hours. Stir occasionally to prevent sticking. Ladle into hot sterilized jars and seal immediately.

PEACHY APPLE JAM

4 cups tart apples,
   peeled, cored, and
   chopped

4 cups peaches, peeled
   and chopped

juice and rind of 1 lemon

7 cups granulated sugar

Combine all ingredients in a heavy saucepan. Cook over medium-low heat until thickened and transparent, stirring often to prevent sticking. Cooking time is approximately 1 hour. Ladle into hot sterilized jars and seal immediately.

APPLE-CINNAMON JELLY

4 cups apple juice

1 pkg (2 1/2 oz) powdered
   fruit pectin

4 1/2 cups granulated
   sugar

1/4 cup cinnamon
   heart candies

Combine juice and pectin in Dutch oven. Bring to a full rolling boil, then stir in sugar and candies. Bring to a full rolling boil again and boil hard for 2 minutes, stirring constantly. Remove from heat, stir, and skim for a few minutes. Pour into hot sterilized jars and seal immediately.

Note: I find that adding 1 tsp butter to jelly and jam mixtures reduces foaming to a minimum.

APPLE JELLY

I like to make apple jelly the old-fashioned way, without added pectin and colouring. Follow these easy directions and you will have perfect, cloudless jelly, with no additives.

Wash apples, removing stems and blossom ends. Slice or quarter. Put apples in a large pot and add enough cold water to barely cover them. Simmer apples until mushy. Drip apple mixture through a double layer of cheesecloth. To do this, I use another large pot and fasten my jelly cloth with several clothespins around the top, pour apple mixture in the centre, and leave it overnight. Do not squeeze the jelly cloth, as this will cause cloudy jelly. (Remember: all that pulp can be put through a sieve for apple butter).

To make up jelly: Use no more than 8 cups of juice at a time. Boil juice rapidly for 3 minutes. Do a pectin test: Combine 1 tsp juice with 1 tsp rubbing alcohol. Let sit a few seconds. If the mixture forms a heavy clot, it's time to add sugar. If it does not clot, boil a few more minutes and re-test. Discard alcohol-juice mixture: DO NOT TASTE, as it is poisonous.

If juice and alcohol have clotted after the first 3 minutes of boiling, add 1 cup granulated sugar to each cup of juice. If you had to boil it a bit longer, add 3/4 cup granulated sugar to 1 cup juice. Boil briskly, uncovered. Remove any scum as it forms.

To test for readiness: Using a cold metal spoon, drip jelly mixture from the spoon back into the pot. If syrup runs in 2 distinct streams, the jelly is cooked. Remove from heat. Let sit 1 minute. Remove any scum with a cold fork or spoon. Pour into hot sterilized jars, and cover with melted paraffin when partially set.

APPLE-MINT JELLY

4 cups apple juice

1 pkg (2 1/2 oz) powdered
fruit pectin

1 cup lightly packed
fresh mint leaves

4 1/2 cups granulated
sugar

green food colouring

Combine juice and pectin in a large pan. Bring to a full rolling boil and stir in sugar and mint leaves. Bring to a full rolling boil again and boil hard for 2 minutes, stirring constantly. Remove from heat, stir in food colouring, and skim for a few minutes. Be sure to skim off all mint leaves. Pour into hot sterilized jars and seal immediately.

APPLE-ROSE JELLY

Rose geranium leaves combine with apple juice in this recipe to make a delicious jelly with a difference.

6 cups apple juice (made
from very tart apples)

1/2 cup lemon juice

10 cups granulated sugar

1 pkg (2 envelopes) liquid
fruit pectin

6–8 washed rose
geranium leaves

Combine juices and sugar in a large pot. Heat to boiling, stirring constantly. When mixture reaches a full rolling boil, stir in fruit pectin all at once and bring again to a full rolling boil. Boil hard for 1 minute, stirring constantly. Remove from heat. Add geranium leaves, and food colouring if desired. Skim off foam and leaves. Ladle into hot sterilized jars and seal immediately. Set in a cool place for 10 days, for jelly to set.

Note: This recipe may be made with commercial apple juice—simply reduce the amount of apple juice used to 4 cups.

DIABETIC APPLE JELLY

This recipe is suitable for most diabetic diets and has only 11 calories per tablespoon.

1/2 pkg (1 envelope) unflavoured gelatin

2 tbsp granulated sugar

2 cups apple juice

1 tsp lemon juice

1 cinnamon stick

6 whole cloves

Combine all ingredients and simmer for 10 minutes. Remove spices. Pour into jelly glasses and refrigerate. Keep in refrigerator. Yields 2 cups.

APPLE MARMALADE

Apples, oranges, and lemons combine to make a lovely marmalade.

8 cups apples, peeled, cored, and finely chopped

1 orange, rind, juice, and pulp

1 lemon, rind and juice

8 cups granulated sugar

Grate rinds from lemon and orange, and extract lemon juice. Add to apples, along with chopped pulp from orange. Discard any white membrane from orange. Combine all ingredients in a large saucepan and simmer until mixture is thickened and apples are tender, approximately 30 to 40 minutes. Remove from heat. Skim, bottle, and seal.

SPICED CRAB APPLES

In this recipe, lightly pricking the apples with the tines of a fork will cut down on splitting of the apple skins.

6 lbs crab apples, with stems attached

1 1/2 cups granulated sugar

1 1/2 cups brown sugar

1 1/2 cups white vinegar

3 cinnamon sticks

1 tbsp whole cloves

Wash apples and cut off blossom ends. Prick with a fork. Combine sugars and vinegar in a saucepan. Tie cinnamon and cloves in a cheesecloth bag. Add to sugar mixture. Bring to a boil, and boil 10 minutes. Add apples, and simmer gently until apples are barely tender. Do not overcook or apples may become mushy. Discard spice bag. Using a slotted spoon, pack apples in hot sterilized jars. Bring syrup to boil and pour over apples. Seal immediately.

APPLE BUTTER

From the kitchen of Marie Howatt of PEI comes an excellent way to use leftover pulp. Unsweetened applesauce also works very well in this recipe.

5 cups apple pulp

7 1/2 cups granulated sugar

1/2 tsp allspice

1 tsp cinnamon

1/2 pkg (1 envelope) liquid fruit pectin

Combine fruit pulp, sugar, allspice, and cinnamon in a large Dutch oven. Bring to a full rolling boil over high heat. Boil rapidly for 1 minute, stirring constantly. Remove from heat and stir in pectin. Stir and skim for 1 minute. Pour into bottles and seal immediately.

Note: 1/2 tsp of butter or margarine, added to the above mixture before cooking, will reduce foaming.

APPLE KETCHUP

12 cups tart apples,
  peeled, cored, and sliced
....
2 1/2 cups onions, finely
  chopped
....
1/2 cup water
....
1 cup granulated sugar
....
1 1/2 cups cider vinegar
....
1 tsp salt
....
1 tsp dry mustard
....
1 tsp cloves
....
1 tsp cinnamon
....
1/4 tsp allspice
....
1/4 tsp pepper
....

Combine apples, onions, and water in a saucepan. Cook until apples are mushy. Put mixture through a sieve. Combine apple mixture with remaining ingredients. Cook uncovered over medium heat until thickened, about 1 hour. Pour into hot sterilized jars, leaving 1/2-inch headspace. Process in boiling water bath for 15 minutes.

Index

OTHER NIMBUS COOKBOOKS:

Favourite Recipes from
Old New Brunswick
Kitchens

Out of Old
Nova Scotia Kitchens

One Potato, Two Potato

The Apple Connection